MAKING
CONCRETE
POTS, BOWLS, & PLATTERS

MAKING CONCRETE
POTS, BOWLS, & PLATTERS

35
STYLISH AND SIMPLE PROJECTS FOR THE HOME AND GARDEN

HESTER VAN OVERBEEK

CICO BOOKS

LONDON NEW YORK

DEDICATION
For my super creative family: my aunts, uncles, and cousins, who always have some DIY advice and tips handy.

Published in 2017 by CICO Books
An imprint of Ryland Peters & Small Ltd
20–21 Jockey's Fields
London WC1R 4BW
341 E 116th St
New York, NY 10029
www.rylandpeters.com

10 9 8 7 6 5 4 3 2 1
Text © Hester van Overbeek 2017
Design and photography © CICO Books
2017

A CIP catalog record for this book is available from the Library of Congress and the British Library.

ISBN: 978 1 78249 414 0

Printed in China

Editor: Gillian Haslam
Designer: Elizabeth Healey
Photographer: James Gardiner
Stylist and step photographer: Hester van Overbeek

In-house editor: Anna Galkina
Head of production: Patricia Harrington
Publishing manager: Penny Craig
Art director: Sally Powell
Publisher: Cindy Richards

CONTENTS

• • •

INTRODUCTION

I love textures—old wood, chipped paint, marble, and concrete are all things I like to work with, so when the opportunity to create this book came along, it got my interest right away.

Concrete is such a lovely medium to work with, but it can have a very industrial image and even my dad said "Are you sure—a whole book of concrete? Isn't that way too difficult for you?" To be fair, you do need to get to grips with a few basic techniques, but mixing and casting concrete is not difficult for the average crafter to master. If you are a novice, I suggest starting with the small projects first—the asymmetric succulent planter on page 28 and the tea light holders on page 90 are very good introductions to concrete crafts. Once you become more confident in creating the perfect concrete mixture, you can start mixing bigger quantities and try the chevron planter on page 20 or the plant table on page 49.

I use a variety of molds for the projects in this book. I've built my own wooden ones, used my silicon baking pans, raided the recycling bin for juice cartons and yogurt pots, and even tried some free casting on sand. Concrete will take any shape you pour it in and will even pick up all the texture inside your molds, so you can get very creative. Most concrete crafts have a strong industrial look, so I also wanted to create some more delicate and unusual pieces, like my doily bowls on page 102, the cake stand on page 76, and the patterned vase on page 114.

Learning how to work with concrete was new to me and I had some disasters along the way—bowls stuck in their molds and mixtures that took forever to set—while running out of concrete mid mega pour and having to dash to the DIY store on a super busy Saturday wasn't one of my highlights! But practice paid off and by tweaking my designs and working out which molds work best, I had a lot of fun and I'm pleased to share my tips and ideas with you here.

I'm not the most patient crafter, and also have a relaxed approach when it comes to making things, but as curing concrete is a chemical process you do have to be quite precise and learn to play the waiting game as you won't know if your cast has worked until a day or so after you made it. However, I had so much fun coming up with some unique projects for you to make and I hope you will become a concrete convert too!

GETTING STARTED

• • •

CHOOSING YOUR CONCRETE

Concrete is a super strong building material, but it is also great for crafts. It is a mix of cement and aggregates, to which you add water to create the exothermic chemical reaction which makes concrete set rock hard.

People seem to mix up the words cement and concrete. To clear it up, cement is the "glue" that holds concrete together. You mix cement with aggregates—such as sharp sand (also called builder's sand), ballast, small rocks, gravel, etc—to make concrete. To make life easy, you can buy packets of premixed concrete, in quick or normal set. Or you can mix your own by combining cement with sand and ballast. On average you mix one part cement with four parts sand/ballast/aggregates, but always follow the instructions on your cement packaging.

I tend to use premixed concrete as it's relatively hassle-free and you only have to add water, but mixing your own is handy if you want a lighter colored concrete. Most premixed concrete is a

gray color, but by using white Portland cement (crushed and finely ground limestone) and colored pigments you can create a lot of different toned projects (see page 71).

Quick-set concrete is also available in premixed packets. This mix will set within an hour—great if you want to make something quickly. Quick-set concrete is perfect for small projects, but I wouldn't recommend it for the large planters as you will not have enough time to mix all the concrete and pour it before the first lot hardens.

Concrete comes in different textures. There are the very smooth and fine ones and the coarser mixes. The coarse ones are cheaper to buy and contain larger pieces of rubble or stones—this concrete is used by builders to make walls, etc. Smoother concrete mixes have finer milled ballast, resulting in a very smooth finish which is great for delicate projects. All brands are different and it's best to try several to see which finish you prefer.

MIXING CONCRETE

Adding water has to be done gradually, a little at a time—you want to end up with a mixture that has the thickness of yogurt. If you make the concrete mix too thin, just add some more concrete powder. Follow the instructions on your concrete packaging to calculate how much water to add.

A common mistake when mixing concrete is to make the mixture too wet. Too much water will result in a poor chemical structure and leaves your projects weak, crumbly, and porous, and it may also shrink while drying in the mold.

Make sure the concrete powder and water are properly combined and no pockets of powder are left. Once all combined, mix for a few more seconds just to be sure you have a good mixture. You will notice the mixture will start to set immediately so you need to work fast, especially if using quick-set concrete. For big projects, mix your concrete in batches and work fast, mixing no more then 17½ lb (8kg) of concrete at a time and only mixing the amount of concrete needed for your project.

Getting the thickness just right can sometimes be a little tricky. A thinner mixture is easier to pour, but don't be tempted to do this as a thin concrete is not as strong as a thicker mixture that you spoon or press into place. Have a look at the mold you use to determine the thickness you need. If you have a mold with lots of details (such as the animal planter on page 52 or the patterned vase on page 114), make the mixture a little thinner so you can pour it into all the crevasses. For your average planter, make your mix the thickness of yogurt so it pours out of your mixing bowl. When you use sand as a mold (see page 63), make your concrete a little thicker so you can pack it into shape without using an inner mold; the same applies to the fruit bowl on page 71.

To make concrete more frost-resistant, it needs to be crack-free and not too wet. Make it as dense as possible for any pieces that will be outside, and if casting, vibrate gently to remove any large air bubbles.

Mixing concrete can look daunting, but don't let it deter you from the creative process of making your own planters and pots. Concrete mixing is a bit like mixing batter for a cake—once you have discovered the perfect thickness for your mix, it will be a walk in the park.

TOP Always wear protective gloves when mixing concrete.

CALCULATING QUANTITIES

All the projects in this book list the approximate weights of the dry concrete mix I used. Use this as a guideline when making your own projects—if you use a similar size of mold, the concrete needed will be almost the same, and you can adjust the quantity if you use a larger or smaller mold.

For those occasions when you find you have mixed too much concrete, I have included some great little projects to use up leftover concrete, such as the dipped cup and saucer on page 74 and the candlesticks on page 80. I also always keep a few recycled yogurt pots on my worktop ready for turning into little concrete planters for succulents!

TOP Kitchen scales are useful for weighing the dry concrete mix.

MOLDS

Molds hold the concrete mix in place until it has set into the required shape. On most projects you will use two molds—one for the outer shape and one as the inner mold, creating the space within your project for plants, flowers, etc.

You can use a wide variety of products as molds. Anything that is hollow can become a mold, so have a good look around your house to see what you have lying around before setting out to buy molds. Most molds are for a single cast but some you can use multiple times, like the wooden frame mold used on page 120.

Silicon Silicon baking pans make great concrete molds. Once the concrete is dry, you can peel the silicon away, making it very easy to release the finished concrete project. Silicon molds have smooth sides, resulting in a smooth project finish, but the walls will bow a bit with the weight of the concrete mix. To prevent this, you can place a piece of wood or a heavy book next to the mold to stop the walls bulging.

Plastic Any plastic shape can be used as a mold, but shapes with a lot of texture or ridges will make it more difficult to release your project once it is dry. You will see me cut off the rims of bowls in some of the projects as the rim can get stuck in the concrete. Bowls or shapes with a little give work

ABOVE Cooking spray will make it easier to remove your finished projects from the mold..

best as something you can pull slightly out of shape makes the concrete easier to release. Very rigid bowls will have to be cut open.

It is wise to spray a releasing agent like cooking spray or olive oil in your plastic mold before pouring the concrete in. This will make it a lot easier to release your project from its mold.

Wood For square, straight, or rectangular projects you can build your own molds from wood. The smoother the wood, the smoother the finish on your project. I like using melamine furniture board—a particle board (sawdust pressed together with glue) that has a smooth resin coating. Pine also works well, but unpainted/unsealed wood will absorb a little water from your concrete mix which can result in a crumbly finish. If you use wood with a pronounced grain, this texture will also appear in your finished project.

ABOVE Silicon baking pans make hassle-free concrete molds.

ABOVE These mini loaf pans are used as molds for the tea light holders shown on the right.

When building molds, make sure all the corners are straight and you fill all the seams with silicon sealant to prevent the concrete mix seeping out. Unmolding is very simple—you just unscrew the screws that hold the wood together.

Wooden molds are perfect if you want to make several planters, pots, etc with the same shape because they can be used over and over again. Just scrape out all the dried concrete residue before using it again.

Recycled Food containers make perfect molds so have a look in your recycling bin for yogurt pots, juice cartons, soda bottles, and milk containers. Plastic drinking cups are great inner molds and unmolding is easy as you just cut the carton open.

Paper You can use cardboard to make molds—this is especially good for swirly shapes like the letter bookend (see page 112). You do have to cover the paper in plastic tape (such as duct tape, gorilla tape, or parcel tape) otherwise the water in the concrete mix will dissolve the paper. Tape the paper mold to a flat surface with strong tape, like duct tape.

Waxed paper, such as juice cartons, make great molds too, as these are already waterproof and don't require any taping (see pages 106 and 116).

LEFT AND BELOW A cardboard mold was used to cast this bookend (see page 112), while sand was used for casting the kitchen trivet (see page 92).

Sand Pouring concrete over sand creates an organic shape, like the serving dish on page 63. The sand will make the negative space and you can really play with swirly shapes, as in the trivet on page 92. If you like a very neat finish, this is not the casting method for you as concrete poured over sand will have a rougher appearance.

When the concrete has dried, simply pull the project away from the sand. Brushing the sand away will take some time. Use a stiff brush, like a dish-washing brush, to rub as much off as you can; letting the sand dry in the sun will also help. If you still haven't got all the sand off, use a steel brush but be careful not to damage the concrete.

Inner molds The inner mold you use will create a negative space (ie the cavity to hold your plants/flowers etc). This mold can be anything that fits easily inside the outer mold. I like using plastic drinking cups, postal tubes, or various plastic containers from my recycling bin. Styrofoam/polystyrene is also good as it can be cut to any shape and makes great knockout pieces for spaces you want to keep clear of concrete, like hanging hooks, watering holes, or planting space. Wine corks make good drainage knockouts too, but they are a bit harder to come by nowadays.

To make it easier to release the inner mold, always make sure it sticks out of the concrete by at least ¾ in (2cm) wherever possible, so it has some pull when you want to remove it.

A releasing agent like a cooking spray, olive oil spray, or mold oil can be use inside the mold to make for easy release. Spray a little inside the mold, especially if the mold has ridges (such as in the storage jar on page 123) before casting your concrete.

ABOVE If the inner mold sticks out above the concrete, it will be easier to remove.

ABOVE Spooning the concrete into the mold and leveling the top.

ABOVE Gently shaking or tapping the mold to level the concrete.

ABOVE Pushing the inner mold into place and tapping the sides to get rid of any air bubbles.

CASTING

You can pour concrete, spoon it into the mold, or pack it in with your gloved hands.

Pouring—where you simply pour the concrete into its mold and smooth it off—is used for most small projects. Poured concrete is often very smooth.

Packing/pressing is great for larger projects and builds that need to hold their shape immediately. The concrete mixture you use is drier and will often create more texture in its walls, like veins and holes.

In some projects, you fill the mold two-thirds full with concrete before pushing the inner mold in, while in others you glue the inner mold to the base and you cast the project upside down (as with the hanging basket on page 24).

Some other pressed projects, like the fruit bowl on page 71, don't even use an inner mold as the concrete mix is strong enough to hold its shape.

After casting, you need to get rid of any air trapped inside your mold. Tap the sides of the mold to release any bubbles that might be trapped in the concrete. When making small projects that are not to heavy, you can also lift the mold slightly and let it drop down again gently on your work surface to remove any air pockets.

The pressure inside the concrete has the tendency to push up your inner mold, so weigh the inner mold down with sand, uncooked rice, screws, nails, or coins to keep it in place.

Make sure your inner mold is centered (unless you have designed something asymmetric) before the curing process starts. You might want to use some lengths of tape to ensure the inner mold stays in place. For big builds, such as the water feature on page 54, the sides of your mold might start to bulge so use planks of wood to keep them straight.

RIGHT Screws are a perfect weight to keep the inner mold in place. You can also use sand, uncooked rice, coins, or nails.

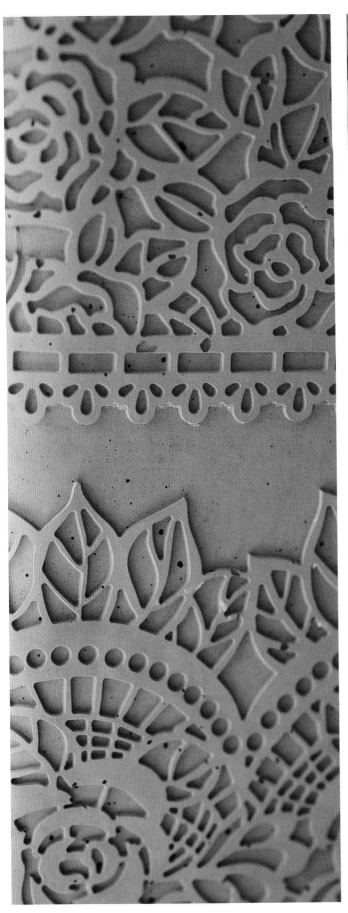

CREATING PATTERNS

Concrete will take on any pattern your mold might have on the inside, like a wood grain or object. When you use a super smooth mold like melamine, a plastic tub, or silicon ice cube tray, your project will be super smooth as well.

You can play with the appearance of your project by adding shapes to the walls of your outer mold. Do this with rubber or foam flowers as in the fruit bowl on page 71, create letters or shapes with silicon sealant as in the chevron planter on page 20 and the candlesticks on page 80, or use silicon textured mats intended for sugar crafting to give great detailed texture to your project, as in the patterned vase on page 114.

You can also tint the inside of your projects with a slurry, as in the fruit bowl on page 71. To make a slurry you mix colored pigment with white Portland cement and water to create a paste the thickness of yogurt which you smear onto the concrete. This will fill any cracks and dips your project may have and give it a smooth colored layer. You can also use this technique to color the outside of a planter, especially ones that have a lot of air bubbles and cracks in the concrete to create a smoother finish.

DRYING TIME

Concrete setting (or curing) doesn't mean drying out the water—it's an exothermic chemical reaction where the water is consumed by the chemical reaction, resulting in a tough material. You will notice the mold getting warm when the curing takes place. When your object feels rock hard and is cold again, it can be time to unmold but if in doubt, always give it a bit longer. I've stated my drying times in the projects, but use your common sense. If you take a project out of its mold before it's cured, it will break.

Small projects, like the succulent planter and candlesticks on pages 28 and 80, can be unmolded after a few hours, larger planters and vases after a full day, and big projects like the chevron planter on page 20 after a few days.

Although your concrete mix will get hard in a few hours or days (depending on its size), it takes weeks for the concrete to fully harden. You will notice the concrete gets lighter the more it cures. Don't worry when you see dark patches when you unmold your projects—these will dry lighter in time.

The slower the concrete cures, the stronger your build, so you can put your mold in a plastic bag or cover a big project with a plastic sheet so it dries a little slower. I especially like

COLORING CONCRETE

Color brings an extra dimension to your project and can either be added into the concrete mix by using pigments or by painting the object after it has been unmolded.

Adding pigments results in an integral color—a color that is dispersed throughout the concrete, not just on the surface. This is great for objects that might have a little wear and tear—for example, when a planter gets chipped the underlying concrete is the same color. Pigments that you add to the concrete mix come in dry and liquid form and although you can use paint pigments (such as in the two-tone bowl on page 96), I've had varied results doing this—some colors worked fine while others made the concrete crumbly. Concrete curing is a chemical process so use pigments specially made for concrete to ensure you don't mess up the chemical reaction.

You can also use gel food colors to add a marbled affect, as in the bookend on page 112. Pour the colors into the base of the mold and swirl them around before pouring the concrete in. You will not know how the color has taken until after unmolding, making this a fun technique. The brighter the pigment and the lighter the concrete, the more it will show up.

Most ready mixed concrete is of a gray color and great for industrial tones, like the phone charging station on page 116, but if you want vibrant colors this gray tone might dull your pigments. In this case mix your own concrete using a white cement, like Portland cement, as the colors will show up a lot more.

Concrete can be painted after unmolding and, unlike the integral method, the color will be just on the surface of your project. You can use all sorts of paint, but I prefer to work with the chalk paints by Annie Sloan as they dry quickly, don't require any preparation, and the colors are not affected by the gray base of the project.

For a super shiny finish (such as the trivet on page 92) or for a project that will contain water (as on page 54) I use tile paint. This is a bit trickier to apply and it has to dry for a full day, but it can withstand water.

doing this with projects with thin walls that can have a tendency to crack, such as the fruit bowl and plates on pages 71 and 86. If possible, never let your project cure in bright sunlight as concrete that dries too fast will crack.

UNMOLDING

When your concrete has set, you can unmold it. This can be very easy when you have a wood frame which unscrews or a flexible silicon cake pan, or a bit trickier when you use a solid plastic mold.

Always make sure the inner mold sticks out of the concrete by ¾ in (2cm) so you have something to pull on. If you have used cooking spray, the unmolding will be easier as well.

For plastic, remove the inner mold by wiggling it and pulling it away from the concrete (or in the case of a plastic cup you can just scrunch it up). Then pull your outer mold away from the concrete a little to release your build, tip it over, and let your project fall out. If this doesn't happen you will need to cut open the mold with a Stanley knife. Do this carefully and a little at a time, using protective gloves to protect your hands from sharp bits of plastic and wearing goggles to protect your eyes from bits of plastic that might fly off.

I always like to let my projects "air" a little after unmolding before painting them. This doesn't have to be long—half an hour is enough.

BELOW Molds with smooth sides make it easy to release your projects.

SEALING CONCRETE

After sanding and then painting your project, you can seal it with a clear varnish to make sure the paint lasts longer. Using a satin finish will give your make a shiny finish. I often prefer a matt look, so opt for a matt finish sealant.

Concrete objects that will be used for food or food storage will have to be sealed with a food-grade sealant (ie one that is non-toxic). Apply one coat, let dry, then apply another coat.

TOOLS AND PRODUCTS NEEDED

Mix your concrete in an old mixing bowl, flexi bucket, or cheap plastic bowl. I like using disposable spoons to mix small projects and a trowel to mix bigger quantities of concrete. I love using flexi buckets to mix my concrete in, and they also make great molds as they have a smooth interior and a lovely round shape.

Small amounts are good to mix in a mixing bowl or bucket. Larger quantities (such as for the chevron planter on page 20) are easier to mix in a large shallow tray. Mixing large quantities of concrete is heavy work —I developed some good muscles working on this book!

Silicon sealant is a must-have when making your own molds. You use it to seal all the seams so no concrete mixture can leak out and also to stick your molds to a flat base. You could also use hot glue for this (I have in some smaller projects), but sealant works a lot faster. Let it dry before pouring your concrete—this can be anything from 15 minutes for a rapid-drying sealant to a few hours for a normal one.

After unmolding you might have some rough edges on your project, which you can sand away with semi coarse sandpaper. If you want to smooth your project, you can use very fine grade paper.

Inner molds often have to be weighted down to stop the concrete mixture from pressing them up to the surface. Sand, uncooked rice, nails, coins, and screws are perfect for this.

Other tools you might need, depending on your project, are something to smooth the concrete (such as a spoon or scraper), screwdriver, drill, saw, tape measure, stanley knife, strong tape, spirit level, and glue.

LEFT Flexi buckets are great for concrete crafts as they have smooth sides and come in many different sizes. I use them for mixing concrete and also as molds, as in the plant table on page 49.
BELOW Some of my concrete mixing tools.

TIPS

• • •

Open packets of concrete mixes and cement should be closed correctly before storing them inside a shed or storage bin. Concrete powder will react with rain or moisture in the air, resulting in big lumps of set concrete in your mix.

• • •

Concrete planters can be left outside year round in temperate climates, and should be frostproof, but cracks can happen in extreme temperature changes or in very cold weather. Don't use a "flow concrete" that builders use to level floors—even though it has a very fine and neat appearance, it is often not frostproof so not ideal for outdoor projects.

• • •

Concrete can hold water when sealed, but water can make the concrete crack. I always use a glass as the negative mold in my vases (see the geometric vase and the patterned vase on pages 106 and 114) and leave it in the concrete when unmolding. The glass will hold the water, making sure your table or work surface stay dry.

• • •

Concrete can be rough and heavy. To protect your table or shelves you might want to stick felt pads or cork underneath your project.

• • •

Leftover mixed concrete can be used for small projects, like the dipped coffee cup and saucer on page 74. Otherwise pour it into a plastic bag or a throwaway container and let it set before disposing of it (some recycling centers will recycle concrete as building waste). Never, ever pour leftover concrete mix down the drain, as it will set and block your pipes.

• • •

Clean molds and mixing bowls by scraping out all the leftover dried concrete before washing with soapy warm water.

• • •

Make sure you work on a stable and level work surface—you don't want to end up with planters with wonky bottoms!

• • •

1

GARDENING
& OUTDOORS

YOU WILL NEED

• • •

furniture board or other smooth
wood, for the mold:

• *four pieces 13 x 15 in (33 x 38cm)
for the sides of the outer mold*

• *one piece 13 in (33cm) x [13 in
(33cm) + twice the thickness of the
wood] for the base of the outer mold*

• *four pieces 8 x 15 in (20 x 38cm) for
the sides of the inner mold*

• *one piece 8 in (20cm) x [8 in (20cm)
+ twice the thickness of the wood] for
the base of the inner mold*

~

measuring tape

saw

silicon sealant

wood drill

screws

screwdriver

strong tape, such as duct tape

piece of cardboard, 2 x 12 in
(5 x 30cm)

glue gun

concrete mix—I used
approximately 55 lb (25kg)

safety goggles, gloves, and
dust mask

cooking spray

sand

palm sander (optional)

hammer

palette knife

sandpaper

CHEVRON PLANTER

• • •

Large concrete planters look great in the garden, and their
sturdy, rustic look goes especially well with plants with bright
flowers or fine leaves, like this date palm. To give your planter
a little bit more interest, give it a chevron motif—this looks
tricky, but is in fact a super simple step as all you need is
a tube of silicon sealant. Be careful, though—you might
get hooked on making your own planters in all different
sizes and patterns!

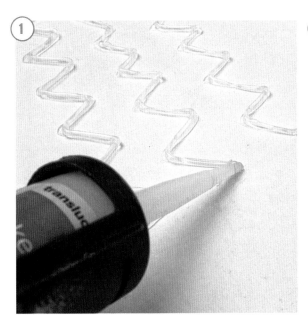

1 Cut your wood to size. Using the silicon sealant, apply a zigzag chevron motif to the four larger pieces of wood that will form the sides of the outer mold, working the lines across from one long edge to the other long edge. Don't take the lines of sealant right to the edges as you need to have enough space at the sides to screw the boards together. Also make sure that the lines of sealant will match up at the edges when the cube is assembled.

2 Pre-drill three holes on each long side of these larger pieces and screw together to make a cube, making sure that the zigzag sealant lines are on the inside. Attach the base of the mold in the same way (i.e. pre-drill holes in line with the point where the sides meet the base and then screw together).

3 Using the silicon sealant, seal the inside joins of the mold around the sides and base so that the concrete will not seep through.

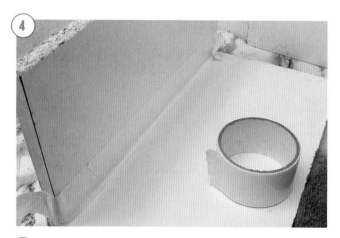

4 Using strong tape, tape together the inner mold. Make sure the tape is on the inside of the mold so you can reach it once the concrete has set. Also attach the base to the sides with tape.

5 Roll the cardboard into a tube and wrap it in tape to make it waterproof. This tube will form the drainage hole for the planter. Glue the cardboard tube in the center of the base of the larger mold using the glue gun.

6 Mix the concrete according to the packet instructions (also see page 9) and pour enough into the bottom of the large mold to reach just to the top of the cardboard tube.

7 Lightly spray the outside (sides and base) of the inner mold with cooking spray. Place the small mold on top of the cardboard tube and fill the mold with sand to make sure it stays in place. I also used some lengths of tape to make sure the mold didn't move. The sides of the inner mold will be higher than the outer mold—this will allow you to remove the inner mold more easily when the concrete has set.

8 Fill the sides between the two molds with concrete. To remove the air bubbles from the concrete mix, either hit the sides of the mold with a flat hand or place a palm sander on the sides for a minute or so. Let the concrete set—this will take a few days.

9 To remove the sides of the inner mold, pull the tape away, then use a hammer to tap the inner boards gently toward the center and away from the concrete. Leave the inner base in place for the moment.

10 Remove the screws around the edges of the outer mold. Run a palette knife along the edges to cut away the silicon sealant and gently prise the boards away from the concrete. Do this to all the sides and the base.

11 Pull out the cardboard tube to reveal the drainage hole, then push up through this hole to remove the base of the inner mold. If any silicon sealant is stuck in the chevron motif, pull this out using your fingers. Give the side and top edges a light sanding if needed, then plant your palm in your new planter.

8

9

10

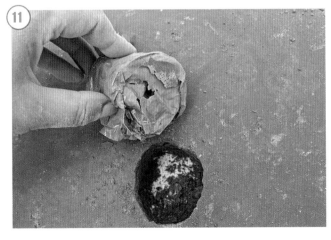

11

TIP

. . .

Planters are a lot of fun to make but as you
have to mix a large amount of concrete, I think
this project is suitable once you have a little bit
of concrete-making experience, so try some of the
other projects in this book first if necessary.

HANGING BASKET

· · ·

Here I love the color combination of gray concrete and purple lavender. Although usually grown in big planters or borders, I thought I would give one of my favorite plants a prime spot in my garden with this hanging basket. An extra bonus of having lavender in a hanging basket is that every time it sways in the wind, its lovely aroma drifts through the garden. To give the basket a unique look, I made the hanging holes triangular instead of round. Combined with the jersey rope, this makes for a very contemporary planter.

YOU WILL NEED

· · ·

2 plastic plant pots, one with a 4½ in (11cm) diameter and the other a 4 in (10cm) diameter

piece of flat wood—I used an old laminate floorboard

glue gun

thick piece of foam

scissors

cooking spray

concrete mix—I used approximately 2¼ lb (1kg)

safety goggles, gloves, and dust mask

craft knife

fine sandpaper

palette knife

lavender plant and potting compost

jersey yarn—I used Hoooked's Zpagetti yarn

1 If your smaller plant pot has a rim, cut it off. Place the small plant pot upside down on the board and use the glue gun to apply a line of glue all around the lower edge. Try to keep the glue line as neat as possible as this will show in the finished basket.

2 Cut three triangular shapes from the foam and glue them to the outside of the pot with one point of each triangle facing down—these will form the hanging holes so space them equidistantly. Make sure the foam is thick enough to touch the wall of the larger pot, otherwise the concrete will seep in between and you will not be left with a hole. Also cut a round piece of foam and glue it to the top of the pot—this will make the drainage hole in the base of the basket.

3 Cut the base out of the larger plant pot. Lightly spray the inside of the outer mold and the outside of the inner mold with cooking spray. Place the larger pot over the smaller one and double check that the foam triangles touch the sides. Glue the lower rim of the pot to the board.

4 Mix the concrete according to the packet instructions (also see page 9) and carefully pour into the mold. Don't allow the concrete to go any higher than the top of the round piece of foam or you will block the drainage hole. Tap the mold to release any air bubbles trapped in the mix.

5 Let the concrete set—this could be a few hours for rapid-set concrete mix or a day for a normal one. When dry, cut away the glue holding the outer plant pot to the board and make a vertical cut in the pot itself to make for easy release. Remove the plant pot.

6 Pull out the foam piece to reveal the drainage hole.

7 Using the palette knife, carefully prise the concrete pot from the board. Work your way around the pot to release the glue.

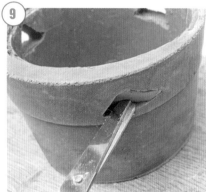

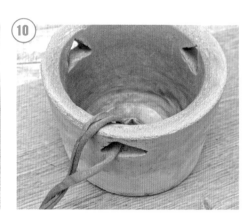

8 Use the palette knife to loosen the inner plantpot from the concrete and pull the pot out.

9 Pull out the triangular foam pieces to reveal the hanging holes—you may need to use scissors to get the foam out. Remove any rough edges on the hanging basket using fine sandpaper.

10 Pick a strong yarn in a color that goes well with your pot—I opted for a blue jersey yarn. Cut three 6-ft (2-m) lengths. Push the yarn through the hanging holes, making sure both ends are the same length.

11 Plant your lavender in the pot. Knot the yarn on the rim of the basket, then tie the six yarn ends together roughly 4 in (10cm) above the plant.

12 Braid three ends of yarn together to create one strong piece. Do the same with the other three ends. Tie the yarn around a sturdy tree branch, pole, or hook to hang the basket.

ASYMMETRIC SUCCULENT PLANTER

• • •

I love succulents, mainly as they seem to be the only plants I am able to keep alive. My whole house is filled with these little fat specimens—I have most of them grouped together in big containers, but some are so pretty it's nice to single them out, for example in this planter. I used picnicware as a mold—you can buy this very cheaply in your pound or dime store. This is where I also found this great triangular-shaped drinking cup, which is perfect for an asymmetric planter. The top is painted in a bright blue chalk paint—you can either apply an all-over color or tape off parts of the planter with masking tape to create the geometric pattern.

YOU WILL NEED

...

cooking spray

plastic bowl and drinking cup, to use as molds

concrete mix—I used approximately
3¼ lb (1.5kg)

safety goggles, gloves, and dust mask

mixing spoon

rice or sand

scissors

fine sandpaper

masking tape

paint—I used Annie Sloan Chalk Paint
in Provence

paintbrush

chalk paint varnish (optional)

small succulent plant and potting compost

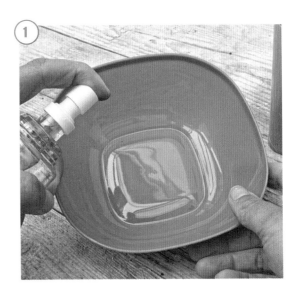

1 Spray the inside of the bowl with a little cooking spray to make sure the dried concrete releases easily.

2 Mix the concrete according to the packet instructions (also see page 9) and pour it in the bowl, filling the bowl about half full. Push the cup in the concrete, making sure it is off-center but at least 1¼ in (3cm) from the edge as you don't want to make the wall too thin. Fill the mold with the rest of the concrete.

3 Fill the cup with rice or sand to prevent it from floating up. Tap the sides of the bowl to release all the air bubbles from the concrete mix. Let the concrete set—this can take about an hour for quick-set concrete or half a day for normal concrete.

4 When the concrete is set, make
a vertical cut in the cup so you can
squeeze its walls in and pull it out
from the concrete. Pull the walls of the
bowl out a little to release the planter
and tip it out of the bowl.

5 Using fine sandpaper, smooth away
any roughness on the edges of the
planter, making sure all the sanding
dust is brushed off before you paint it.

6 Cut the masking tape into triangles
(or any other shape you want). Stick
the masking tape shapes in a random
pattern on your planter, working
outward from the planting hole. Also
apply masking tape to the sides of the
planter to keep it clean of paint drips.

7 Give the top of the planter a coat
of paint and allow to dry thoroughly.

8 When the paint is dry, peel off the
pieces of masking tape. If you wish,
apply a coat of clear varnish to make
the paint more durable. Allow to dry,
then plant the succulent in the hole
and water sparingly.

YOU WILL NEED

...

a large drinking cup, at least 6 in (15cm) high and 4 in (10cm) wide

craft knife

a smaller drinking cup that fits inside the larger one with ease

large drinking straw, ½ in (1cm) in diameter

tape

a flat surface, such as a tray or piece of wood

silicon sealant

cooking spray

concrete mix—I used approximately 1 lb 2 oz (500g)

safety goggles, gloves, and dust mask

putty knife

sandpaper

paint

paintbrush

plant/landscape fabric (the type used for weed control), 14 x 6 in (35 x 15cm)

needle and thread

2 pieces of metal wire, each 12 in (30cm) long

scissors

sponge, 2½ x 2½ in (6 x 6cm)

plant and potting compost

metal ring, ¾ in (2cm) in diameter

string, for hanging

UPSIDE-DOWN PLANTER

• • •

Why grow your plants the right way up if they can hang upside down? Upside-down planters have become popular, especially for air plants, but did you know it's not at all tricky to make your own? And how cute do the polka dots look! These two look great against my garden shed, but would look equally attractive indoors. The hole on the top of the planter makes it easy to water the plant, while the sponge inside the planter will retain water and keep the potting compost in place.

1 Cut away the base of the larger cup using the craft knife.

2 Make a mark in the center of the base of the smaller cup, cut a smaller hole, and push the straw through. Keep the straw in place with some tape.

3 Place the smaller cup on the flat surface, rim down, and glue it in place using the silicone sealant. Place the larger cup around it and seal that in place as well. Let the sealant harden for an hour. Lightly spray the inside of the mold with cooking spray. Mix the concrete according to the packet instructions (also see page 9) and pour into the mold, filling it about ¾ in (2cm) above the inner mold. Tap the sides to release any air bubbles.

4 Let the concrete dry—this will take anything from a few hours to a day. When hard, carefully peel away the outer cup. Prise the concrete planter away from the flat surface using a putty knife, then pull out the straw and the inner cup. Don't worry if the inner cup is stuck—you can leave it in place and still use the planter, but ideally take it out.

5 Sand away any rough edges on the planter and brush away any sanding dust. Give the outside of the planter a coat of white paint. When dry, paint on the colored polka dots.

6 Fold the plant cloth in half widthways and sew the two sides together using running stitch. This will create a cloth "bag" with an open top edge.

7 Fold over the open top edge of the bag by ½ in (1cm), to create a double thickness. Weave one piece of metal wire through the folded-over top edge from one side seam to the other. Repeat on the other side with the second piece of wire.

8 At the two side seams wrap the pieces of metal around each other and cut off one long length, so you have two pieces of metal wire left over.

9 Cut a small hole in the center of the piece of sponge. Also cut a small cross in the bottom of the fabric bag.

10 Carefully push the leaves of the plant through the hole in the sponge, then through the slit in the base of the fabric bag. The sponge should now be pushed up next to the base of the fabric bag.

11 Fill the rest of the bag with the potting compost. Pull the metal wire almost closed —don't completely close it or the water won't get in.

12 Push the metal wire through the hole in the base of the planter and pull the bag inside, so that it sits snugly inside the planter.

13 Wrap the metal wires that come through the planter base around the metal ring, then tie some string to the ring and your planter is ready to be hung.

TIP

• • •

Water the plant through
the hole at the top (upside
down planters are best
for plants that only need
light watering).

VERTICAL GARDEN

• • •

Picking home-grown herbs is any cook's idea of bliss. Even if you don't have a garden or a balcony, you can still achieve this with this stylish vertical garden. Filled to the brim with basil, chives, parsley, oregano, and mint, this concrete planter will not only look great on your kitchen counter but also add a hint of country flair. You could also use this planter for other plants, such as succulents and cacti. Use a spray bottle to water your herbs or place the planter flat on the floor for a good soak from a watering can.

YOU WILL NEED

...

plywood, ⅝ in (1.5cm) thick—see step 1 for sizes

measuring rule

saw

drill

screws and screwdriver

rubble sack or strong plastic sheet

staple gun

chicken wire

8 corner squares

a smooth plank for the mold base, 30 x 15 in (75 x 38cm)—I used furniture board

a plank for the mold sides, 1¾ in (4.5cm) wide, cut into two 30 in (75cm) lengths and two 16 in (40cm) lengths

silicon sealant

concrete mix–I used approximately 40 lb (18kg)

safety goggles, gloves, and dust mask

trowel

spoon

plants and potting compost

1 Cut your plywood to size. You will need one piece 12 x 10 ⅝ in (30 x 27cm) for the base, two side pieces 12 x 3½ in (30 x 8.8cm), and another two side pieces 9½ x 3 ⅜ in (24 x 8.5cm).

2 Predrill holes in the large plywood base piece, ½ in (1cm) from the corners. Screw from the base into the side pieces to create a box (this will eventually hold the plants and potting compost).

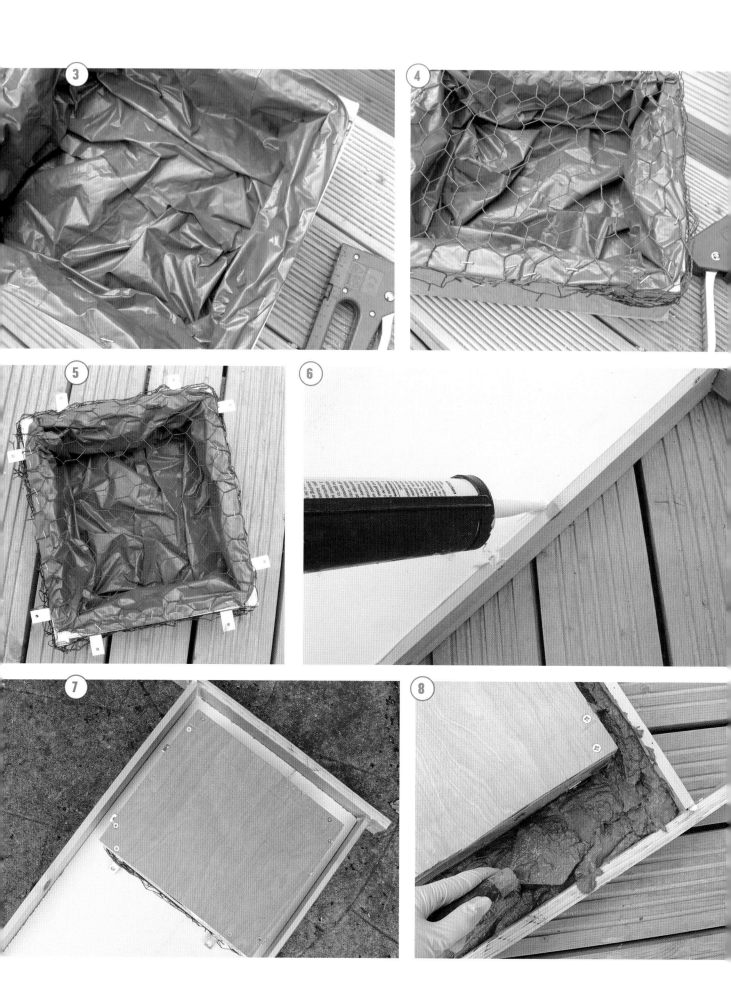

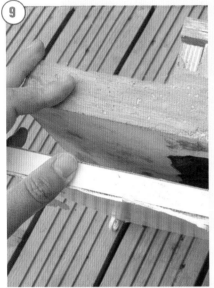

9

10

11

3 Cut a piece of plastic to fit inside the box and staple in place around the rim of the box.

4 Cut a piece of chicken wire 2 in (5cm) larger than the box. Staple in place, folding the edges over the rim and down onto the sides.

5 Attach the corner squares ¾ in (2cm) in from each corner and ¼ in (5mm) from the front of the box (these metal pieces will help the box grip to the concrete, but if you have them completely flush to the front of the box they will show).

6 Now construct the mold for the concrete. Screw the mold side pieces into the mold base to create a large rectangle. Seal the joints to make sure no concrete will leak out.

7 Place the box in the mold, chicken-wire side down, positioning the box at least 2 in (5cm) down from the top edge.

8 Mix the concrete according to the packet instructions (also see page 9). This is a large quantity, so mix in two buckets. Press the concrete into the mold. Fill the mold up completely and smooth the top as much as you can. Let harden for a few days.

9 When the concrete has set, unscrew the mold and remove the side pieces. Carefully prise the concrete away from the base of the mold.

10 When you turn the concrete over, you will see that the edges of the wooden box are not completely concealed by the concrete. Mix a little extra concrete and "paint" this over the wood using a spoon. Let harden.

11 Half-fill the box with potting compost, feeding it through the chicken wire. Snip the chicken wire where you want to place the plants, then push each plant through the wire and firmly into the potting compost. Fill the space between the plants with more potting compost. Give the plants a good watering before you stand your vertical garden upright.

RECYCLED
PLANTERS

● ● ●

Your recycling bin is a treasure trove when it
comes to sourcing molds. Empty yogurt pots,
milk and soda bottles, and potato chip canisters
make perfect casting vessels. The planters seen
here have a rough edge as they have been cast
with pebbles, little rocks, and sand, giving them
a textured appearance. They look great grouped
together, planted with different succulents and
cacti—more of these planters can be seen in the
photo on page 18. As these planters don't have
a drainage hole, they are best for plants that only
need a tiny bit of water at a time.

YOU WILL NEED

...

empty pots, cups, and bottles in a variety of
shapes and/or sizes (including some smaller
ones for the inner molds)

scissors

cooking spray

concrete mix—the quantity depends on
the size of planter, but allow roughly 9 oz
(250g) per planter

safety goggles, gloves, and
dust mask

little stones, rocks, and/or sand

pieces of broken china (optional)

PLASTIC BOTTLE MOLD

1 Cut a plastic soda bottle in half 6 in (15cm) up from the base. Spray the inside of the bottle with cooking spray.

2 Mix the concrete according to the packet instructions (also see page 9). Fill the base of the bottle with concrete, then place some small stones or rocks on the concrete.

3 Pour some more concrete on top of the stones until the mold is half full, then push a plastic drinking cup into the middle of the mold.

4 Fill the cup with sand to stop it rising up. Also sprinkle some sand on top of the concrete for added texture. Allow the concrete to dry thoroughly, then pull out the inner mold and carefully cut open the bottle. Brush the excess sand off the rim.

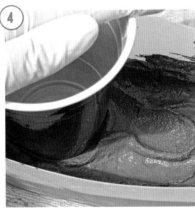

MILK CARTON MOLD

1 Cut open a large plastic milk carton 4 in (10cm) up from the base.

2 Smash up an old bowl, plate, or cup so you have some patterned shards.

3 Mix the concrete as above. Fill the base of the mold with concrete and place the ceramic shards along the outside edge (place the patterned side against the milk carton).

4 Fill the rest of the mold about three-quarters full with concrete until all ceramic pieces have been covered. Push two plastic cups down into the concrete. To stop them rising up, either weigh them down with a heavy book or a long length of sticky tape (see page 23). Allow the concrete to dry thoroughly, then pull out the cups and carefully cut open the milk carton.

BIRDHOUSE

• • •

Let the local birds live in style in this lovely birdhouse, or as one of my friends said "surely it's a bird bunker as it's made of concrete!" How nice would this birdhouse look in your garden or on your balcony? Don't be put off by the number of steps as this build is really not that difficult to make. The wooden door slots into the concrete house due to its tapered shape—there's no need to screw it in, just push it in place.

YOU WILL NEED

•••

two round plastic pudding bowls, one 1 pint (570ml) and one 2 pints (1.15 litres)

craft knife

paper and pen

glue

¼ x ¼ x ⅝ in x (5mm x 5mm x 1.5cm) piece of styrofoam/polystyrene

cooking spray

concrete mix—I used approximately 1 lb 10 oz (750g)

safety goggles, gloves, and dust mask

nails or coins, to use as a weight

old spoon

small piece of the wood for the door— I used plywood ¼ in (6mm) thick

1 in (2.5cm) circle cutter and/or jigsaw

sandpaper

small piece of dowel, ¾ in (2cm) long and ¼ in (5mm) thick

drill and wooden drill bit

wood glue

paint and paintbrush

8 x 10 in (20 x 25cm) piece of wood for the back—I used pine board ¾ in (2cm) thick

saw

D-ring picture hook

two little screws, for attaching hook

screwdriver

bolt, 2 in (5cm) long and ¼ in (5mm) thick

three ¼ in (5mm) washers

¼ in (5mm) nut

1 The bowls need to be tapered in shape with the circumference of the top rim bigger than the bottom. These pudding bowls are perfect. Carefully cut the rim off the smaller bowl with a craft knife—this will make it easier to get the mold out of the concrete later.

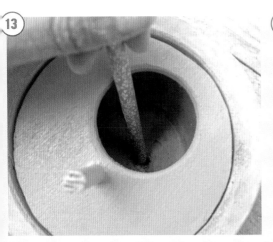
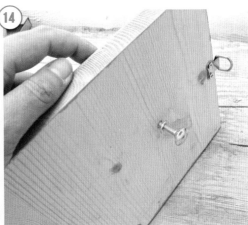

2 Place the small bowl on a piece of paper and draw around it. Keep to one side as this will form the template for the wooden door.

3 Glue the piece of styrofoam to the base of the bigger mold, positioning it in the center and standing on one end. This will create the hole for the bolt in the back of the concrete birdhouse.

4 Lightly spray the inside of the bigger mold and the outside of the inner mold with cooking spray. Mix your concrete according to the packet instructions (also see page 9) and fill the mold until the styrofoam just peeks out.

5 Place the inner mold on top of the styrofoam and weigh it down with nails. Spoon the concrete between the inner and outer molds, filling the gap to the top. Smooth the concrete down as much as you can and make sure the whole mold is filled. Tap the bowl to get rid of any air bubbles. Let the concrete set.

6 Cut out the circle drawn onto the paper and transfer to the plywood. Draw another smaller circle inside—this will form the entry hole for the birds. Cut out the inner circle using the circle cutter. If you don't have a circle cutter, drill a hole in the middle of the circle to fit your jigsaw blade and cut out that way.

7 Cut out the door using a jigsaw. Sand away any rough edges.

8 The dowel forms a perch for the birds. Mark its position on plywood, then drill a hole the same size as your dowel. Glue the dowel in place with wood glue.

9 Paint the board and the door of the birdhouse and let dry. Apply a second coat if necessary.

10 When the concrete has set, remove the inner bowl—you may need to cut it a little to be able to remove it. Run a knife between the concrete and the outer mold. When it loosens, tip the mold upside down and release the concrete from the pudding bowl.

11 Push the piece of styrofoam out of the concrete. Sand away any rough edges. Check that the door fits inside the birdhouse, and sand down a bit more if necessary.

12 Screw the picture hook to the middle of the top of the board, fixing it to the reverse side.

13 Place the birdhouse on the board (I like mine positioned toward the top of the board) and mark where the drill hole needs to go.

14 Drill a hole ¼ in (5mm) in diameter. Put a washer around the bolt and push from the back through the wooden board.

15 Put another washer on the other side and then put the birdhouse in place. Apply the last washer and then the nut. Tighten the nut to secure the birdhouse to the board. Push the door in place and your birdhouse is ready to be hung.

COPPER PLANTER WITH SAUCER

• • •

Most planters need a dish beneath them to catch water from the drainage hole but this can often spoil the look of your planter, so why not make a matching saucer? Painted in copper paint and made from a very light concrete, this planter will look super stylish on your mantelpiece, table, or bookcase. I made mine in a small microwave tub and it's just big enough to hold a medium-sized succulent, but you can of course play around with the size and make yours as small or as large as you wish.

YOU WILL NEED

...

three circular 19 fl oz (550ml) tubs—mine are 4¾ in (12cm) wide and 3¼ in (8cm) high

measuring tape

pen

craft knife

piece of baking parchment

silicon sealant

strong tape

concrete mix—I used approximately 1 lb 5 oz (600g)

safety goggles, gloves, and dust mask

nails or coins, to use as a weight

large plastic drinking cup—I used a 17fl oz (500ml) one

scissors

sandpaper

copper paint

paintbrush

masking tape

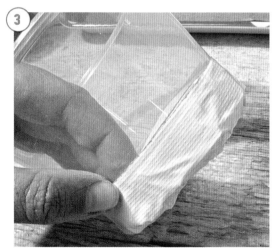

1 Draw a line all around one of the tubs, 1 in (2.5cm) from the bottom. Cut along this line and discard the bottom part of this tub.

2 Place the cut piece on a piece of baking parchment on a flat surface and stick in place with silicon sealant.

3 Wrap the bottom 2 in (5cm) of another tub in strong tape, padding the tub out by about ¼ in (5mm) all around.

4 Apply a blob of silicon sealant roughly ½ in (1cm) tall to the middle of the third tub—this will create the drainage hole. Let the sealant harden.

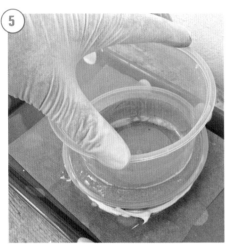

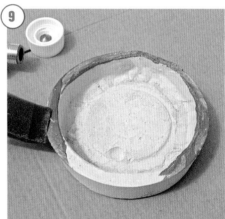

5 Mix your concrete according to the packet instructions (also see page 9) and fill the saucer mold half full. Place the padded-out tub in the middle of the saucer mold and weigh down with nails, screws, or coins. Let the concrete set.

6 Fill the base of the third tub so the sealant blob just peeks out. Place the cup on the sealant and fill the rest of the mold with concrete. Weigh the cup down with nails or coins and let the concrete set.

7 When the concrete saucer is dry, pull the sealant away from the outer tub, squeeze the inner tub, and pull out of the mold. Turn upside down and push the saucer out of its mold, then squeeze the cup and pull it out of the concrete.

8 When the concrete pot is dry, pull the drinking cup out of the pot, then cut the tub open with scissors and release the pot. Push the sealant blob out of the concrete base.

9 Sand away any rough edges. Paint the saucer with copper paint—you will probably need two coats but let the paint dry thoroughly between layers.

10 Apply a strip of masking tape ¾ in (2cm) from the rim of the pot and paint the top section with the copper paint—you probably need two coats here as well. I chose to leave the rest of the pot as plain concrete. When the paint is dry, remove the tape.

PLANT TABLE

• • •

Show off your plants and flowers on this plant table. With a smooth concrete top and copper legs, this table is so on trend and would look good in any living room, whether your style is Scandi chic, bohemian, or industrial. Cutting copper pipes is so much easier than it looks—all you need is a pipe cutter that you simply twist around the pipe to cut it to size. You could just push the table legs into the concrete but trying to get them level would be tricky, so building the frame first results in a strong and stable table. You'll find the copper pipe and the various joints in the plumbing section of your local building store.

YOU WILL NEED

...

two copper pipes, 6 ft (1.8m) long and ⅝ in (15mm) in diameter

pipe cutter

measuring rule

two ⅝ in (15mm) equal T joints (shaped like the letter T)

four ⅝ in (15mm) elbow joints

four ⅝ in (15mm) end pieces

strong glue suitable for use with metal, such as Gorilla Glue

concrete mix—I used approximately 17½ lb (8kg)

safety goggles, gloves, and dust mask

flexible bucket, 13½ in (34cm) high, 18 in (45cm) in diameter at the top rim and 15 in (38cm) in diameter at the base

trowel

large chopping board or flat piece of wood

spirit level

sandpaper

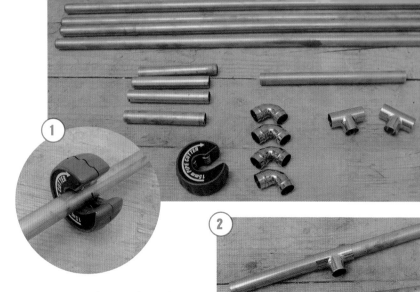

1 Cut your copper pipes to size using a pipe cutter. Mark where your cut needs to be, push the cutter around the pipe, and twist around until the cut is made. You need four 22 in (55cm) pieces, four 4 in (10cm) pieces, and one 7 in (18cm) piece.

2 Glue two 4 in (10cm) pieces to the opposite ends of an equal T. The easiest way is to put a drop of glue inside the equal T's opening. Repeat with the other equal T and the remaining two 4 in (10cm) pieces.

3 Connect the two pieces you have just created with the 7 in (18cm) piece. Glue in place to make an H shape.

4 Glue the elbow pieces to the pipe ends. Do this on a table and make sure your corners are all pointing straight up at the same angle. Let the glue harden, then glue the legs into the elbows. You may have to prop the legs up with books or a bucket to make sure they dry in a straight line. Let the glue set.

5 Mix your concrete according to the packet instructions (also see page 9) and put half of the mix in the base of the bucket. Place the copper frame on top of the concrete in the middle of the bucket.

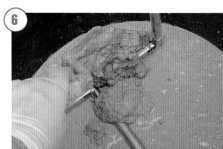

6 Place the remaining concrete on top and around the frame. Tap or gently shake the bucket to release any air bubbles and smooth the surface of the concrete as much as you can.

7 To check your base is still level before the concrete sets, place a flat chopping board or piece of wood across the leg ends and place a spirit level on top. Adjust the angle of the pipe base if necessary. Leave the concrete to set.

8 When the concrete has set (this will take about a day), pull the sides of the tub away from the table. When all the sides are released, you can simply pull the table out (if this doesn't work, cut the tub open).

9 Smooth away any rough edges on the underside of the table with sandpaper. Glue the pipe ends to the ends of the legs. You can bend the pipe legs out a bit to make for a nicer shape and to level your structure if needed.

ANIMAL PLANTER

• • •

Who doesn't want a Theodorus the Tortoise in their life? Any hollow soft plastic toy, such as the ones used at children's bathtime, can be turned into a planter—just make sure the head, or any other part of the body, isn't any higher than where the plant would go otherwise the concrete may not fill the mold properly. Perfect toy molds are tortoises, crocodiles, bugs, and other "flat" animal shapes. Theodorus the Tortoise looks great with a cactus or succulent planted in his back—as he doesn't have a drainage hole, this planter is best suited for plants that don't need regular watering.

YOU WILL NEED
...

hollow soft plastic toy—this tortoise is 6¾ x 3¼ in (17 x 8cm)

marker pen

craft knife

silicon sealant

concrete mix—I used approximately 10½ oz (300g)

safety goggles, gloves, and dust mask

piece of paper or foil

small yogurt pot—I used one 2 x 1½ in (5 x 4cm) and 1½ in (4cm) deep

nails or coins, to use as a weight

strong glue (optional)

sandpaper (optional)

small plant and potting compost

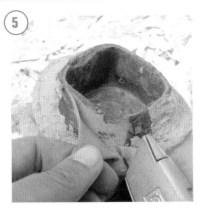

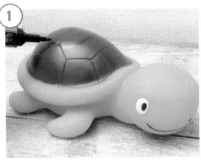

1 On the top of your animal's back draw a circle with a diameter to match the yogurt pot. Carefully cut out the circle using a craft knife.

2 Most plastic toys have an air hole in the bottom—close this with a blob of silicon sealant.

3 Mix your concrete according to the packet instructions (also see page 9) and pour into the tortoise (place the mold on a piece of paper or foil as it will get messy). Squeeze the mold to make sure the head and legs are completely filled with concrete.

4 Push the yogurt pot in place and weigh down with some nails or coins. Don't worry about any concrete which spills out onto the top of the mold. Let the concrete set thoroughly.

5 Squeeze the yogurt pot to release it from the concrete and pull it out. Cut the plastic mold so you can peel it away from the concrete. Take extra care with the feet/tail as they will be more fragile. One foot and the tail of my planter were stuck in the mold—if this happens, just glue them back on using a strong glue.

6 The top of the tortoise's head was slightly higher than its back and that top bit didn't fill with concrete, leaving a small air bubble. I don't mind this and left the edge of the dip rough, but you can sand the edges if you prefer a neater finish. Put some potting compost in the hole and add your plant.

WATER FEATURE

• • •

There is just something so relaxing about the background sound of running water. If you don't have space in your garden for a pond, why not make this water feature? It's big enough to hold a small pump and some plants and flowers, but small enough to sit at the end of your outdoor table or on your terrace. The concrete box is rather heavy, so make sure your table can take its weight. The pump is a small fountain that comes with different attachments to control the flow of the water. You can buy pumps that are solar powered or run on mains electricity (always make sure you use an outdoor waterproof socket for the electric one).

YOU WILL NEED
...

two plastic storage boxes, one 14 x 10 in (35 x 25cm) and a smaller one 10 x 6¾ in (25 x 17cm)

saw

flat surface, such as a wooden board or metal sheet

silicon sealant

cork

strong glue

concrete mix—I used approximately 44 lb (20kg)

safety goggles, gloves, and dust mask

strong tape, such as duct tape

stanley knife

corkscrew or knife (optional)

palette knife

sandpaper

masking tape

white tile paint

paintbrush

pump for a small pond or container—I used a Sunspray SE360 pump

water plants—I used a water hyacinth and some grass

1 Cut the base out of the larger storage box—it is easiest to do this using a saw. Place the bottomless box on your flat surface and stick in place with silicon sealant.

2 Stick the cork to one of the sides, roughly 4 in (10cm) up from the base (this will be the hole for the pump cable). Mix your concrete according to the packet instructions (also see page 9) and fill the storage box to a depth of at least 1½ in (4cm).

3 Using your hands (and wearing protective gloves), pack more concrete onto the sides of the mold.

4 Place the smaller storage box into the middle of the mold, taking care not to dislodge the cork. Pack the sides with concrete—I made my concrete box 5½ in (14cm) high.

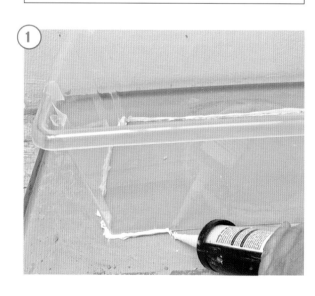

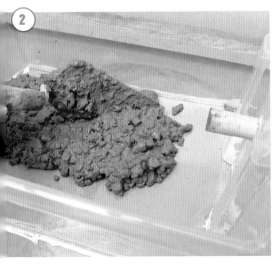

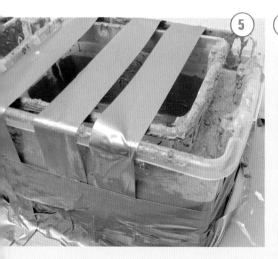

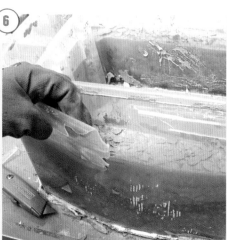

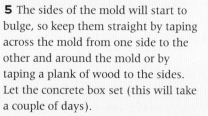

5 The sides of the mold will start to bulge, so keep them straight by taping across the mold from one side to the other and around the mold or by taping a plank of wood to the sides. Let the concrete box set (this will take a couple of days).

6 Cut away the sealant around the base of the mold using a stanley knife. Cut open the outer mold—you need to wear protective goggles and gloves for this as the shards of plastic can be very sharp.

7 Pull out the inner mold—it should release after a few wiggles. Push the cork out of the concrete. If it is stuck, use a corkscrew or a knife to get it out.

8 Release the concrete box from the flat base by running a palette knife underneath it., then sand away any rough edges.

9 Paint the inside of the base with tile paint. I used a shiny white as this will make the water look so much nicer then the gray concrete color. (You could try an aqua tile paint for a tropical feel.) Apply masking tape to the top so you keep the top and sides clear. Allow the paint to dry—this may take a whole day.

10 When the paint has dried, remove the masking tape and push the pump cable through the cork hole. Position the pump in its place and fill the hole around the cable with silicon sealant. Let the sealant dry completely before filling the base with water.

11 Position the plants, switch on the pump, then sit back and relax listening to the sound of the flowing water. You can also float some flowerheads in the water for a pretty finishing touch.

2

FOOD &
ENTERTAINING

CHEESE BOARD

• • •

I love sharing foods, with a big platter placed in the middle of the table so everybody can help themselves to tasty treats. I serve snacks in this way when having friends over for drinks and also at dinner time—it's just so much more social when everybody eats from the same platter. This concrete food board will certainly make a statement with its robust look. It is great for cheese and crackers, charcuterie, or crudités. The board is sealed with a concrete sealant so the food juices will not seep into it—simply wipe clean after use or wash gently with soap and lukewarm water. Use the board for serving rather than as a chopping board, as a knife may scratch the concrete (although some sealants are scratch resistant).

YOU WILL NEED

...

cardboard

scissors

ruler

packing tape

wooden board—I used an old laminate floorboard

jars or cans, to use as weights

strong tape, such as duct tape

concrete mix—I used approximately 4½ lb (2kg)

safety goggles, gloves, and dust mask

large plastic bag

decorating knife or a putty knife

fine sandpaper

food-grade concrete countertop sealant

old cloth

short length of rope

1 Cut the cardboard into strips 4 in (10cm) wide and cover them with tape to make them water/concrete resistant. Join the pieces together with tape to make a strip roughly 32 in (80cm) long (depending on the size of board you want to make).

2 Place the long strip on the board and manipulate it into your chosen shape. I chose an asymmetrical oval with a handle, but a rectangle or circle would also work well. Use cans or jars to keep the cardboard in its shape. Use the stronger duct tape to tape the cardboard to the board. Make sure you tape all the way around so there are no gaps for concrete to seep out.

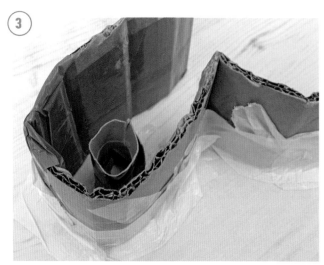

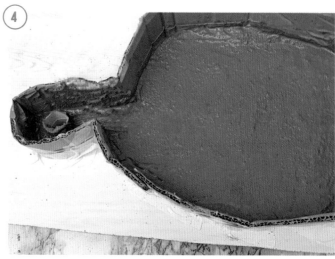

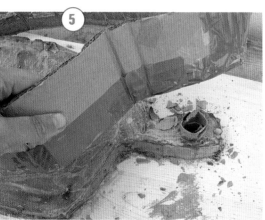

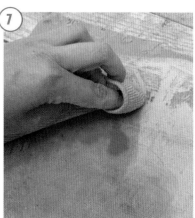

3 Fold a small piece of tape-covered cardboard into a tube and tape or glue it to the base of the board to create a hole in the handle for the rope to go through.

> ### TIP
> ...
> If the concrete is allowed to dry slowly over a longer period, this will make for a stronger cheese board. This is important for a project like this, which will have a lot of handling. Placing it in a plastic bag while drying means that it doesn't lose moisture too quickly.

4 Mix the concrete according to the packet instructions (also see page 9) and pour into the mold to a thickness of roughly ¾ in (2cm). Try to get the mixture as level and smooth as possible. Tap and gently shake the board to release any air bubbles from the concrete. Cover the board with a plastic bag (you don't want it to dry too quickly—see tip), and let it set for at least 48 hours.

5 Pull or cut away the strong tape and pull the cardboard away to reveal your board. Also pull out the cardboard in the neck of the board—it should come away easily.

6 Use a knife to prise the board away from the laminate. Lift it off and you will see the bottom of the board is super smooth—this side will be the top of your board. Use a fine sandpaper to remove any rough edges on the sides. Brush all the sanding dust away.

7 Cover the board with a coating of food-grade sealant, following the instructions on the tin (I had to rub mine in with a cloth). Let the sealant dry, then apply a second coat if needed. Tie a piece of rope through the hole in the handle and your board is ready to be laden with treats.

SERVING DISH

• • •

Concrete can be cast over sand as well as in molds. The sand adds texture to your piece and this freeform method of pouring creates pleasing organic shapes. Every piece will be unique as you never know how the concrete will move. Adding glass mosaic pieces to this serving dish injects it with a little color and fun. The tiny mosaic squares remind me of "dolly mixtures"—the cutest name ever for a sweet candy I first encountered when I moved to the UK.

YOU WILL NEED
• • •

large shallow box, at least
18 x 10 in (45 x 25cm)

sand—I used building sand, but
any sand will do

colored glass mosaic pieces

concrete—I used approximately
5½ lb (2.5kg)

safety goggles, gloves, and
dust mask

trowel

food-grade concrete sealant

paintbrush

1 Fill a shallow box half full with sand. If your sand is too dry, add a little bit of water—you need just enough for the sand to hold its shape when molded.

2 Mold the sand into a smooth dome shape roughly 15 in (38cm) long, 3¼ in (8cm) high, and 7 in (18cm) wide.

3 Place the mosaic pieces on the sand, pushing them in just a little so they stay in place when the concrete is poured. Don't press them too deeply into the sand as they need to be level with the concrete. Make any pattern you like.

4 Mix your concrete according to the packet instructions (also see page 9), making it a little thicker than normal (you don't want it too runny). Place the concrete mix on top of the dome.

5 Use a trowel to smooth the concrete down over the sides. Don't press too hard to avoid dislodging the mosaic pieces. Make the base of the dish level as you don't want it to wobble. Also smooth down the sides as much as you can.

6 Let the concrete set, allowing a few days to completely harden. Carefully pull the concrete dish away from the dome and scrape out all the sand. Use a brush to get all the sand out of the dish; if the sand is damp, it can help to let the dish dry out for a while in between brushing.

7 Coat the dish with two layers of concrete sealant, letting the first coat dry thoroughly before applying the second coat.

CONCRETE TRAY

• • •

This rectangular tray is perfect for serving cold drinks, arranging candles on, or carrying breakfast to the table. The dark blue band contrasts well with the gray of the concrete and the handles make it very easy to use. A concrete tray will be a bit heavier than a wooden or plastic one, but it makes such a style impact. I used foil baking trays as molds as they are very easy to peel off the concrete once it has set. If you would like to make a round tray, use a pie case but just make sure the rim is thick enough to set the handles in.

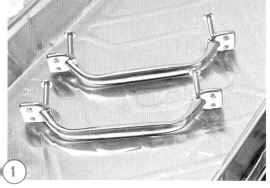

YOU WILL NEED

...

2 foil baking trays, one slightly smaller than the other

2 door handles, slightly smaller than the width of the larger baking tray (plus the fixing bolts for the handles)

concrete mix—I used approximately 6¾ lb (3kg)

safety goggles, gloves, and dust mask

a piece of thick cardboard that fits inside the smaller foil tray

sand

fine sandpaper

paint and paintbrush

1 Insert the fixing bolts into the ends of each handle.

2 Mix the concrete according to the packet instructions (also see page 9). Pour it into the larger foil tray until it is two-thirds full. Put a piece of thick cardboard in the base of the smaller tray and fill with sand. The cardboard ensures that the inside of the tray will be flat and the sand prevents the tray floating up. Place the smaller tray in the middle and push it down evenly so the sides of the outer tray fill up with concrete.

3 Push the handles in place—the bolts make sure the concrete has something to adhere to, ensuring they stay in place when you hold the tray. Tap the tray to release the air bubbles from the concrete and let the concrete set for a day or so.

4 Pull the smaller foil tray out of the concrete. Also peel away the sides of the larger foil tray. You should now be able to lift the concrete tray out of the foil by its handles.

5 Remove any rough edges using fine sandpaper and brush away the sanding dust. Paint the rim of the tray dark blue (one coat should be enough). Let the paint dry and your tray is ready to use.

FIRE BOWL

• • •

Nothing beats a long summer evening spent outside with friends, chatting, listening to music, and watching the sun set. When dusk approaches, light this great fire bowl for its glow and warmth. The flames come from a tin of fire gel that sits safely inside your handmade bowl, hidden from sight by ceramic pebbles (the ones used in a gas fireplace). This piece surely gets the conversation going and sets the scene for a great garden party.

YOU WILL NEED

• • •

small flexible rubber bucket or tub, to use as a mold

plastic bowl that fits inside the bucket, to use as a mold

cardboard and tape (optional)

cooking spray

concrete mix—I used approximately 11 lb (5kg)

safety goggles, gloves, and dust mask

rice or sand

brick, or similar heavy object

fine sandpaper

tin of fire gel

ceramic fireplace pebbles

1 Your finished bowl needs to be large enough to hold the tin of fire gel, so bear this in mind when choosing your molds. The inner bowl should have a base which is about a quarter of the bucket's base, to allow your finished bowl to have a thick wall. The bowl I used as the inner mold wasn't tall enough so I made the sides higher with cardboard (wrap the cardboard with tape to make it water resistant).

2 Spray the inside of the bucket with cooking spray to make sure the bowl will come out easily. Mix the concrete according to the packet instructions (also see page 9) and pour into the tub, filling it two-thirds full.

TIP

• • •

Make sure you only use ceramic pebbles specially designed to be used in this way. Don't be tempted to collect pebbles from the beach instead—the moisture in these would expand when hot and may cause the pebbles to explode.

FIRE SAFETY

- Always keep the bowl away from low branches, parasols, bunting, etc.
- Don't allow the bowl to burn unsupervised.
- Watch the bowl if children and pets are around.
- Blow the fire gel out when you are finished or use a snuffer.

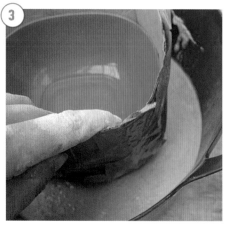

3 Place the bowl in the middle of the concrete and press it down. Tap the sides of the bucket to release any air bubbles from the concrete.

4 Fill the bowl with rice or sand to keep it weighed down. I also added a plastic tub and a brick on top to make sure the bowl didn't move while the concrete was drying. Let the bowl set for a few days.

5 When the concrete is dry, remove the weights and gently pull the inner bowl away from the concrete.

6 Pull the rim of the bucket away from the concrete to loosen the bowl and place the bucket upside down. You should be able to peel the tub away

from the concrete very easily now. If you can't, you might need to cut the tub. Sand any rough edges with fine sandpaper until you have a smooth finish, then brush the dust away. There's no need to sand the inside of the bowl as this will be hidden by the fire gel and pebbles.

7 Place the tin of fire gel inside the bowl, leaving the lid closed until you are ready to light it. Arrange the pebbles on and around the tin, hiding it as much as you can. To light the bowl, follow the instructions on the tin of fire gel (also see the fire safety notes on page 69).

FRUIT BOWL

• • •

This rough-cast concrete bowl is given a softer edge by the flower motifs cast in the outside. The motifs were created by sticking foam flowers around the inside of the mold. You could, of course, use foam letters, animal shapes, or circles (look in the kids' sections of craft stores for a huge array of foam shapes). The purple slurry mix gives the inside of the bowl a touch of color, making your green apples look even greener.

YOU WILL NEED

• • •

foam flowers, available from craft supply stores

plastic bowl, 12 in (30cm) in diameter

glue (optional)

cooking spray

concrete mix—I used approximately 4½ lb (2kg)

safety goggles, gloves, and dust mask

large plastic bag

craft knife

sandpaper

mixing bowl and spoon

3½ oz (100g) white Portland cement

purple pigment

sponge

1 Stick the foam flowers to the inside of your bowl. Most foam shapes have adhesive backs which make this very easy, otherwise use glue. I doubled up some of the flowers to create more depth in the pattern. When finished, lightly spray the inside of the bowl with cooking spray for easy release when the concrete has set.

2 Mix the concrete according to the packet instructions (also see page 9). It needs to be a little thicker then normal —aim for the thickness of Greek yogurt. Using gloved hands, press the concrete against the inside of the bowl, as high as you want your bowl to be. The sides of the bowl need to be about ⅝ in (1.5cm) thick, and the base about 1 in (2.5cm) thick.

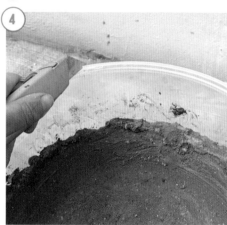

3 Smooth the inside of the bowl as much as you can, then place it in a plastic bag. The bowl needs to dry slowly to make it less likely to crack. Leave to dry for a couple of days.

4 When the concrete has set completely, make some vertical cuts in the rim of the plastic bowl. Wearing protective gloves and goggles, break the top pieces of plastic away.

5 When you see movement in the bowl, tip the mold upside down to release the bowl. You will now see the indentations left by the foam flowers. Sand away any rough edges and brush away the sanding dust.

6 To make the slurry, mix the Portland cement with 2 tablespoons of pigment (or less or more depending on the depth of color you want to achieve) and some water into a paste—again, aim for the thickness of Greek yogurt.

7 Using a sponge, apply the slurry to the inside of the bowl. The slurry will add color and hide any unevenness, such as veins or little holes. Let the slurry dry, then carefully sand away any rough edges.

CUP AND SAUCER

• • •

This is a great project if you have any mixed concrete left over from another make. The cup couldn't be any easier to make and for the saucer you only need a small amount of concrete mix. This stylish set would sure brighten up your coffee break. The cup is hand wash only—don't be tempted to pop it in the dishwasher or all your crafty concrete will disappear. Only wash the inside of the mug, trying not to get any water on the concrete part.

YOU WILL NEED

...

white ceramic coffee mug

leftover concrete mix—I used approximately 1 lb 2 oz (500g)

safety goggles, gloves, and dust mask

sheet of plastic

sandpaper

varnish or clear sealer

paintbrush

plastic plant saucers in two different sizes, to use as molds

spoon (optional)

rice or sand

white paint—satin or chalk paint is ideal

1 For the mug, dip the lower half of the cup in the concrete mix, then place it on a sheet of plastic to dry. The cup will harden very quickly as the layer of concrete is so thin.

2 If there are any bumps on the base of the cup, rub them down with sandpaper to ensure that the cup doesn't wobble. Seal the concrete with a varnish or sealer to make sure the concrete dust doesn't rub off on your hands every time you use it.

3 For the saucer, pour a small amount of concrete into the larger saucer. Push the smaller saucer into the middle, applying a little pressure so the concrete comes up at the sides. I left the top edge rough, but if you like a smoother finish run the back of a spoon over the concrete for an even look.

4 Place rice or sand in the smaller saucer to stop it from rising up. Let the concrete harden—this will take a few hours.

5 Remove the upper plant saucer and gently tip the concrete saucer out of its plastic mold. Sand away any rough edges. Brush off any sanding dust before painting.

6 Paint the inside of the saucer with white paint (I left the outer rim as plain concrete, which I sealed with a coat of varnish). Let it dry thoroughly.

CAKE STAND

• • •

Here industrial-looking concrete is given a feminine look
by partnering it with glass and soft curves. Adding a glass
pedestal to the cake stand and giving the top a scalloped
edge produces a softer, girly look. Who knew concrete and
cake could look so good together? I used a glass candlestick
for the cake stand foot, but a small vase would work
just as well.

YOU WILL NEED
...

silicon sealant

silicon pie dish, 6¾ in (17cm) in
diameter and 1¼ in (3cm) deep

concrete mix—I used
approximately 1 lb 5 oz (600g)

safety goggles, gloves, and
dust mask

spoon

glass candlestick, 6 in (15cm) tall

spirit level

sandpaper

food-grade concrete sealant

paintbrush

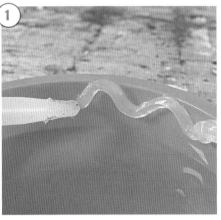

1 To create the scalloped edge, pipe a swirling line of silicon sealant around the inside of the pie dish, with the swirls reaching from the middle to the top edge of the dish.

2 Fill in the space above the swirls with silicon sealant so the concrete will form a pretty scalloped edge. You might want to apply two layers of sealant to make it really thick. Let the sealant dry for an hour or until it feels firm.

3 Mix the concrete according to the packet instructions (also see page 9) and pour half the mix into the pie dish, placing it toward the scalloped edge. Use a spoon or your fingers to push the concrete up the sides following the line of the silicon. Make sure you don't cover the silicon or you will lose the scalloped effect.

4 Pour the rest of the concrete into the dish—you need the concrete to be at least ¾ in (2cm) thick. Smooth the

surface, then shake or tap the dish to release any air bubbles. Do this quickly as the concrete will set fast. Push the candlestick into the center of the dish, ensuring it is level otherwise you will have a wonky cake stand (use a spirit level to check). Make sure you don't push the candlestick right through the concrete to the base of the pie dish, or you will see the edge of the candlestick in the top surface of the cake stand. Let the concrete harden.

5 When fully dry, carefully peel the pie dish away. If some of the edges aren't sharp enough or if some of the concrete leaked over the silicon scallops, define the rim a little more by sanding away any extra pieces of concrete.

6 Paint the concrete with a coat of food-grade sealant to make the cake stand safe to use with food. I like to apply two layers, letting the first layer dry thoroughly before applying the second one.

COASTERS

• • •

If you are new to working with concrete, then this is a great project for you! As the coasters are small, you don't need to mix too much concrete at once and it's great practice for learning how to pour and smooth out the concrete mix. For an experienced concrete master, this is a handy project if you have concrete mix left over from other makes. Using an empty potato chip canister as a mold, the coasters are big enough for drinking glasses; if you like using larger cups and mugs, you will need a bigger mold—you could try using a postal tube instead.

YOU WILL NEED

• • •

potato chip canister, 3 in (7.5cm) in diameter

measuring tape or ruler

scissors

strong tape, such as duct tape

flat, smooth surface, such as a piece of wood or serving tray

concrete mix—I used approximately 1 lb 2 oz (500g)

safety goggles, gloves, and dust mask

plastic knife (optional)

sandpaper

paintbrush and paint—I used Annie Sloan Chalk Paint

masking tape

concrete sealant (optional)

protective felt or cork pads

glue

1 Cut your canister into circles 1¼ in (3cm) deep (you will need six circles for six coasters). Tape the circles to your smooth surface.

2 Mix your concrete according to the packet instructions (also see page 9) and pour into the molds. Smooth the surface of the concrete using your fingers or a plastic knife—you want it to be completely level.

3 Let the concrete set. When hard, peel away the tape and cut open the circular molds. Sand away any rough edges. Brush away any sanding dust.

4 Paint patterns on the top of the coasters. If you wish, use masking tape to create color blocks. Use as many colors per coaster as you like. Leave to dry.

5 When the paint is dry, you may wish to seal the coasters with concrete sealant to make the paint last longer. Glue felt or cork pads to the base of the coasters to prevent scratches on your table.

CANDLESTICKS

• • •

These candlesticks are so easy to make—you will have a whole collection in no time! You can cast them plain or with letters or numbers imprinted on the sides. Wouldn't they make great alternative birthday candles? I used silicon sealant to write numbers 1, 2, and 3 inside the molds as well as letters X, O, X, O, as we all need kisses and cuddles at times!

YOU WILL NEED

...

silicon ice cube tray—I used an extra-large one with 2 in (5cm) cubes

silicon sealant

concrete mix—I used appoximately 2 lb 3 oz (1kg) for 6 candlesticks

safety goggles, gloves, and dust mask

candle cups

sandpaper

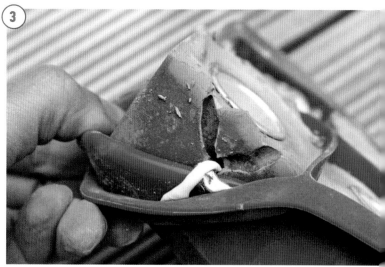

1 Find an ice cube tray that is big enough to hold the candle cups. Using silicone sealant, write letters or numbers on the insides of the molds. Remember you have to write mirrored, or back to front (you might want to practice on paper first).

2 Mix the concrete according to the packet instructions (also see page 9) and fill the molds almost to the top, then tap the sides to release any air bubbles. Push a candle cup in the middle of each mold before the concrete gets too hard.

3 When the concrete has set (this takes a day or so), carefully peel the mold away from the concrete cubes and sand away any rough edges.

CANOPY WITH LIGHTS

• • •

This pretty canopy is stable and windproof due to its concrete feet and can be left outdoors all year round. It frames the outdoor table perfectly and brings atmosphere and light to a barbecue party. I love the big bulbs of these outdoor string lights, but smaller fairy lights would look amazing as well. You could decorate yours with lanterns, streamers, solar lights, bunting, or flags as well. You could even make two structures and stretch a cloth canopy between them to create a shady spot above your picnic table.

YOU WILL NEED

•••

three dowels, 6½ ft (2m) in length and ⅝–1 in (16–25mm) thick

measuring tape

saw

two flexi tubs or buckets, 8¾ in (22cm) in diameter

cooking spray

concrete mix— I used approximately 35 lb (16kg)

safety goggles, gloves, and dust mask

trowel

masking tape

palette knife

stanley knife

sandpaper

white satin paint and paintbrush

two short T-clamps, 1 in (2.5cm) wide

four screws and a screwdriver

string lights suitable for outdoor use

1 Saw the dowels to make two pieces 74 in (190cm) long and one piece 63 in (160cm) long.

2 Lightly spray the inside of the tubs with cooking spray. Divide the dry concrete mix evenly between the two tubs. Working one tub at a time, add water to the dry mix according to the packet instructions (also see page 9) and stir well until you have a yogurt-like thickness. Repeat with the second tub. The depth of concrete in each tub is about 4¼ in (11cm). Push a long dowel into the middle of each tub and use masking tape to make sure it stands upright in the center. Leave the concrete to set (this takes a few days).

3 When the concrete has set, run a palette knife around the top of the concrete to loosen it from the tubs.

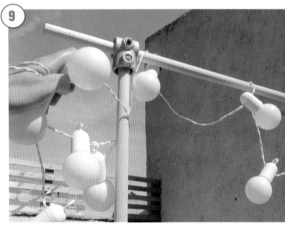

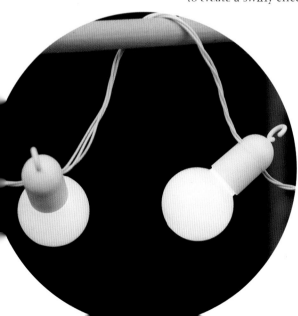

4 Try to pull the concrete away from the tubs, otherwise cut the tubs open with a stanley knife.

5 Sand away any rough edges, brush the dust away, and use masking tape to create stripes on the base. I love the look of hand-painted stripes so I applied the tape in a very relaxed way to create a swirly effect.

6 Apply white paint to the sides of the two concrete bases. Also paint the tops of the bases. Let dry and apply a second coat if needed. Remove the masking tape.

7 Screw the T-clamps to the top of the upright dowels.

8 Slide the shorter dowel through the opening of the T-clamps and screw in place.

9 Your canopy is now ready to be decorated with lights. Make sure your lights are for outdoor use and if they use electricity, make sure you use an outdoor plug. You could also use solar-powered lights.

CHARGERS

• • •

These concrete plates don't just look stylish, they also protect your table from marks caused by warm dishes. They are cast in a pie dish, with the paper liner adding texture to the rim of the plates. If you prefer a smoother look, you can either sand these away or don't use the liner at all. Using a quick-set concrete mix means you can make a whole batch of these plates in just one day.

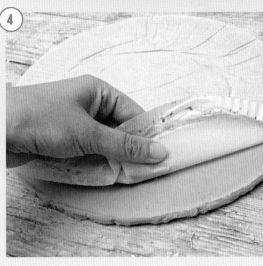

YOU WILL NEED

...

pie pan, 12 in (30cm) in diameter, loose-bottomed or springform

paper pan liner

concrete mix—I used approximately 1¾ lb (800g) per plate

safety goggles, gloves, and dust mask

plastic spatula or knife

sandpaper

food-grade concrete sealant (optional)

TIP

...

This is a very good starter project if you haven't worked with concrete before.

1 Line your pie pan with a paper liner, making the base as smooth as possible. Mix your concrete according to the packet instructions (also see page 9) and pour it onto the liner to a depth of about ⅜ in (8mm).

2 Smooth the concrete as much as possible using a plastic spatula or a knife, then tap the pie pan to release any air bubbles from the concrete. Gently shaking the mold also levels the concrete nicely.

3 Let the concrete set (see instructions on the packet). When hard, release the base of the pie pan.

4 Peel the liner away from the plate. I love the rougher edges on the plate, but if you prefer a smoother finish you can sand these down. If you want to use these chargers for serving food, give them a coat of food-grade sealant.

DOWEL BREAD BASKET

• • •

This dowel bread basket is a great mix of '70s retro and industrial chic. The dowels are set in the concrete base and accented with brightly colored jersey yarn. Use one color of yarn as I have, or create a striped pattern with two or more colors. You might even want to go rustic and use garden twine instead. This dowel basket would be great for fruit storage as well, or make a smaller version to hold eggs.

YOU WILL NEED

• • •

five pine dowels, ⅜ in (9mm) in diameter and 35in (90cm) long

measuring tape

saw

sandpaper

paint—I used Annie Sloan Chalk Paint in Versailles

paintbrush

round pie pan, 9½ in (24cm) in diameter

paper liner, the same size as your pie pan

concrete mix—I used approximately 3¾ lb (1.75kg)

safety goggles, gloves, and dust mask

old spoon or plastic glove

food-grade concrete sealant

jersey yarn—I used about 11 yards (10m) of Zpagetti yarn by Hoooked

scissors

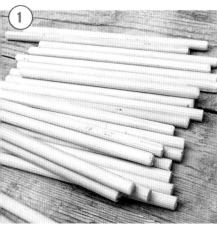

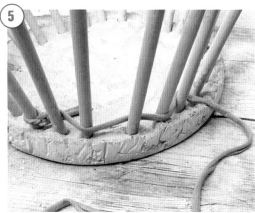
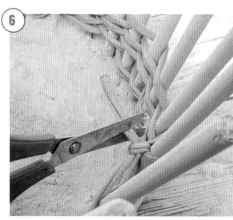

1 Cut the dowels to 7 in (18cm) lengths and sand the edges. Each 35 in (90cm) dowel will create five shorter pieces. Paint all the dowel pieces. Let dry and apply a second coat if needed.

2 Line the pie pan with a paper liner —this will create texture on the sides and makes it easy to release the basket from the mold. Mix your concrete according to the packet instructions (also see page 9) and pour into the pie pan to a depth of about 1¼ in (3cm).

3 Quickly press all 25 dowels into the concrete, ½ in (1cm) in from the edge. Set them at a slight outward angle, evenly spaced around the pan. Smooth the concrete behind the dowels as best as you can, using a gloved finger or spoon. Let the concrete set.

4 Pull the basket out of the pie pan and remove the paper liner. Sand away any rough edges. Seal the concrete with a coat of food-grade concrete sealant and leave to dry.

5 Knot one end of the yarn tightly to one of the dowels. Start weaving the yarn around the dowels, making sure you alternate the rounds. If you wrap the yarn around a dowel on the outside on the first round, then the second wrap goes around the inside of the second round.

6 When you have created the desired height (for me that was seven rounds of weaving), cut the yarn and tie firmly in place.

7 Leaving a gap of 2 in (5cm), repeat the weaving to create a second band of yarn. This time I wove eight rounds. Cut the yarn and tie in place, weaving the ends through the woven yarn to hide them.

TEA LIGHT HOLDERS

• • •

These tea light holders have a very robust look and would look as good on a coffee table as they would in an outdoor dining spot. The concrete is tinted with a sage-green pigment, resulting in a pleasingly deep color. You can use pigments in any tone to color your makes. Just remember that the lighter the concrete mix, the more your color will show. This green is mixed with a gray-toned concrete; if you use a Portland cement mix, the green will stand out a lot more. I found the pigment stained my hands after the tea lights were made, so gave them a coat of clear varnish to lock the color in.

YOU WILL NEED

• • •

2 small loaf pans, 5 x 2¼ in (13 x 6.5cm)

concrete mix—I used approximately 1¾ lb (800g)

safety goggles, gloves, and dust mask

⅞ oz (25g) sage green pigment—I used one by Cemcraft

cooking spray

old spoon

tea light holders

nails or coins, to use as a weight

sandpaper

clear varnish

paintbrush

tea lights

1 This amount is for two tea light holders—if you want to make just one, halve the amount of concrete and pigment. Grease the pans with some cooking spray. Mix the concrete powder with the pigment and add water according to the packet instructions (also see page 9).

2 Spoon the concrete into each mold until almost full. Tap the sides of the pans to release any air bubbles and to level the concrete.

3 Push a tea light holder into each pan, about ¾ in (2cm) from one end. If the holder floats up, weigh it down with some nails and let the concrete set.

4 When the concrete is dry (this will take about 12 hours), tip the pans upside down and tap to release the concrete from the molds.

5 Sand away any rough edges. Coat each tea light holder with clear varnish and let dry completely before popping a tea light into the holder.

TIP

...

This is a great project if you're new to concrete crafts. And if you don't have small loaf pans, you could use an empty sardine tin as long as it's deeper than the candle insert.

KITCHEN TRIVET

• • •

This trivet will bring some rustic charm to your dining table and protect its surface from hot pans at the same time—a win-win situation! Because it is cast in sand, you can make any shape you like. I opted for a flower but a geometric shape would look just as stunning. The metal wire inside the petals strengthens the concrete, allowing you to make delicate shapes as well. I wanted my flower to be super shiny so used white tile paint on the top—this is a very thick paint that will take a full day to dry, but the result is amazing.

YOU WILL NEED

...

metal wire, ⅛ in (3mm) thick and 10 ft (3m) in length

shallow large box, at least 12 x 12 in (30 x 30cm), filled with sand to a depth of 3¼ in (8cm)

old spoon

concrete mix—I used approximately 1 lb 14 oz (850g)

safety goggles, gloves, and dust mask

brush

sandpaper

white tile paint

paintbrush

adhesive cork or felt pads (optional)

1 Fold the length of metal wire in half (you use it doubled), then bend into a shape you like, such as this flower.

2 Place your metal shape on the sand and trace around it to create an outline in the sand.

3 Using the handle of a spoon, deepen and widen the traced line—you want the shape to be 1¼ in (3cm) deep and ¾–1¼ in (2–3cm) wide.

4 Mix your concrete according to the packet instructions (also see page 9) and fill the indentation in the sand half-full. Push your metal shape into the concrete and fill the shape with the rest of the concrete.

5 Push the concrete down firmly to make sure you have a strong bond. Smooth the top of the concrete as much as you can and let it harden for a day or so.

6 When the concrete is set, dig the flower out of the sand. Brush the sand from the concrete. Getting all the sand off might take a while—I let my flower dry in the sun in between brushing. Sand away any rough edges.

7 Decide which side of the flower you want to use as the top. Paint the top of the flower white (I kept the flower center clear of paint). Let the paint dry thoroughly. If you are worried that the trivet may scratch your tabletop, fix a couple of cork or felt pads to the underside.

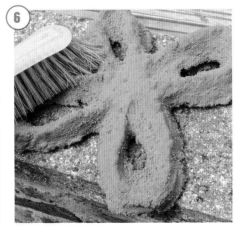

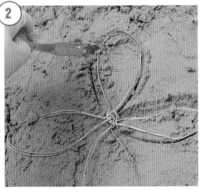

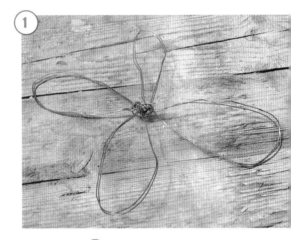

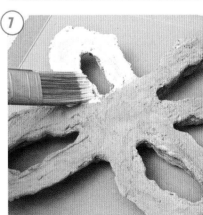

3

DISPLAY
& GIFT

TWO-TONE DECORATIVE BOWL

• • •

Concrete doesn't have to be gray—by using paint pigments you can color the mix and create these great two-tone bowls. You can, of course, paint a plain bowl to create a colored effect, but this method blends color within the concrete and has a textured finish. On the yellow bowl I used a rough sandpaper to create a different texture below the smooth top, so it's not only a two-tone but also a two-textured bowl. The tall vase on page 98 is made with leftover bits of colored concrete "painted" onto the wall of the mold to give a speckled effect.

YOU WILL NEED

...

2 different sizes of foil pie cases for the blue bowl (or 2 different sizes of plastic drinking cups for the green bowl and tall vase), to use as molds

concrete mix—I used approximately 2¼ lb (1kg)

safety goggles, gloves, and dust mask

containers, for mixing the colors

old spoon

paint pigments or liquid cement color

rice or sand, to use as a weight

scissors

fine and rough sandpaper

1 Make sure the foil cases fit inside each other with at least ½ in (1cm) of space between the sides of the bigger and smaller foil cases.

2 Mix the concrete according to the packet instructions (also see page 9) and pour some into the mixing container. Stir in the paint pigment, starting with a little and adding more until you have the depth of color you want—it's a bit like adding food color to cake batter!

3 Pour the colored concrete in the base of the prepared mold, filling it to a depth of about a quarter.

4 Pour the plain concrete on top of the colored one until the mold is two-thirds full. Place the smaller foil case in the center and press it down evenly until the sides have filled with the concrete mix.

⑤

⑥

5 Fill with the smaller mold with rice or sand to weight it down. Let the concrete set for a day or however long it says on the concrete packet.

6 Peel away the foil from the concrete. Remove any rough edges with fine sandpaper and use a rougher paper to add more texture to the colored areas if you wish.

TIP

• • •

I had more success with some colors than others, but it's fun to play around with the pigments. Colors will show up better in white concrete so I used Portland cement mixed with white sand, but you can, of course, use any concrete or cement mix you like. Use specific concrete pigments for guaranteed success.

VARIATION

For the speckled vase, use leftover colored concrete and "paint" it on the inside of the larger plastic cup. You can use a spoon for this or your hands (just make sure you wear gloves). Then continue from step 3.

WOOD AND CONCRETE BOWL

. . .

I love mixing textures and this bowl is a good example, where pouring a concrete rim onto a wooden bowl creates a whole new piece. I would use the bowl as an art object, taking pride of place on my bookcase, but you could use it to store items—it would make an ideal place to keep balls of yarn, trinkets, or keys. The mold is made from duct tape which gives the finished concrete an attractive handmade appearance. I used a fruit bowl made from olive wood, but any round or oval shaped bowl will work well as long as the rim is thick enough to drill small holes in.

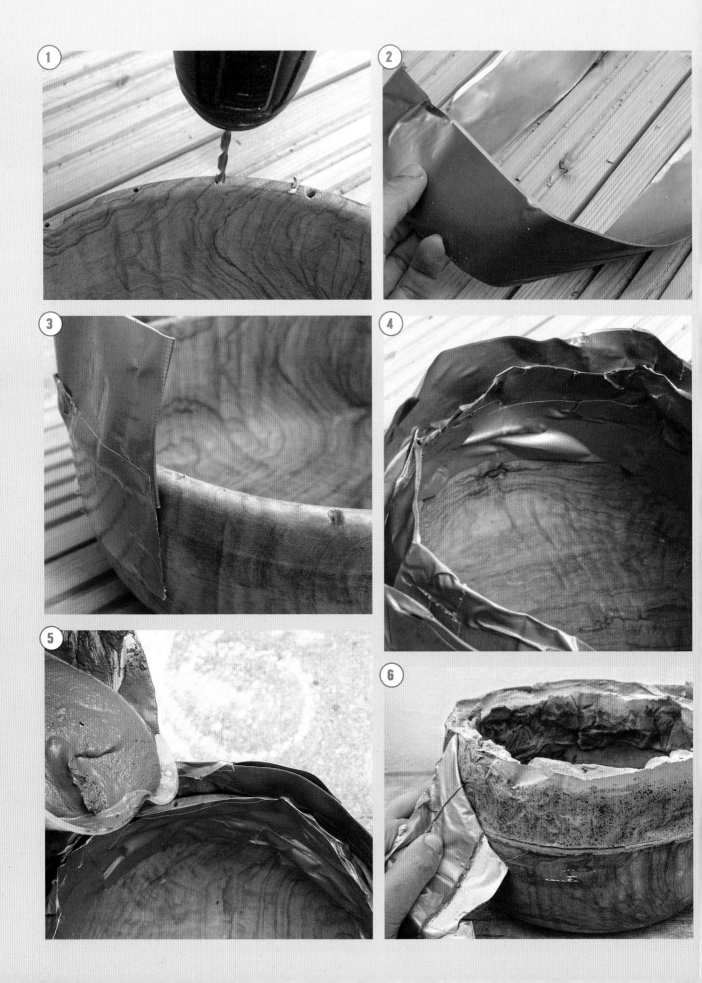

YOU WILL NEED

...

wooden bowl—mine is 8¾ in (22cm) in diameter

drill and ⅛ in (3mm) wooden drill bits

strong tape, such as duct tape

scissors

concrete mix—I used approximately 2 lb 3 oz (1kg)

safety goggles, gloves, and dust mask

sandpaper

1 Drill little holes around the rim of your bowl—the concrete rim needs something to grip to otherwise it will slide off. I predrilled my holes first using the smallest drill bit and then enlarged them to make ⅛ in (3mm) holes.

2 Double up the duct tape, sticking the sticky sides together. Make several strips 8 in (20cm) long.

3 Using another piece of tape, stick the doubled-up tape around the rim of your bowl. Make sure the doubled-up tape sits just on the rim. Continue doing this until the whole outside is covered.

4 Do the same on the inside of the bowl. To ensure the tape mold is strong, add extra layers of tape wherever they are needed.

5 Mix the concrete according to the packet instructions (also see page 9) and carefully pour it into the narrow gap between the two rows of tape. Leave to set for a day or two.

6 When the concrete has set, carefully peel away the tape. Sand away any rough edges that you don't like.

DOILY BOWLS

• • •

Who knew concrete could be so delicate? When thinking of concrete bowls and planters you probably imagine industrial chic, robust and bulky gray builds, and square containers. Well, think again! Using a more liquid concrete mix allows you to soak fabrics and drape them in any shape you like. I thought it was fun to use two polar opposites: the granny-chic doily, normally associated with old-fashioned tea rooms, and concrete, its robust and industrial counterpart. I think it's a match made in heaven! The large bowl is great as a fruit bowl, while the concrete for the bowl shown below was diluted to show off its delicate crochet texture. Due to this, it's a show piece only, but it's a great ornament for display.

YOU WILL NEED

• • •

plastic, to protect your work surface

picnic bowl or ramekin

cooking spray

glass jar

cotton doilies

concrete mix—I used approximately
1 lb 2 oz (500g)

safety goggles, gloves, and dust mask

old mixing bowl

old spoon

fine sandpaper

shallow tray, large glass jar, and knife,
if making the delicate bowl on page 105

VARIATION

1 Use a piece of plastic or a shopping bag to protect your work surface as this is a messy project. Find round shapes to use as molds—I used a picnic bowl for my big bowl, but a ramekin would work well for a small bowl. Spray the outside of your bowl with cooking spray and place it upside down on top of a glass jar to raise it up.

2 Make the concrete mix acording to the packet instructions but with more water than you would usually use—you want the consistency of heavy (double) cream (see also page 9). Submerge the doily in the mix, making sure it's completely covered.

3 Drape the doily over the bowl, folding the fabric around the bowl to create interesting corners and shapes.

4 Leave the doily bowl to set for a day before carefully removing the mold. Use a fine sandpaper to gently sand away any unwanted bumps.

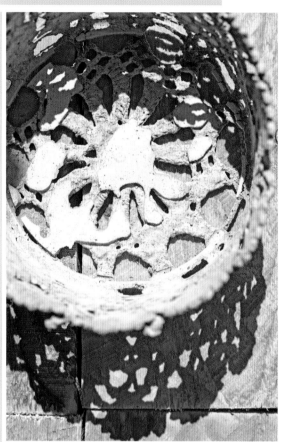

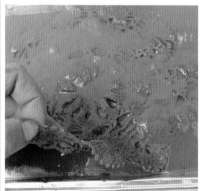

1 For the more delicate bowl, follow steps on the left but after step 2 give the doily a gentle bath in a shallow tray of water to wash out a little of the concrete and reveal the delicate texture of the doily. Don't wash out too much otherwise your bowl won't set.

2 Mold the doily around the base of an upturned glass jar (I used a large gherkin jar). Once dried, run a knife between the jar and the bowl to release the bowl, taking care as this bowl is very delicate.

GEOMETRIC VASE

• • •

I love this pale pink vase! With its smooth sides and geometric shapes, you might assume it would be super hard to make but in fact all you need is a juice carton and some creative folding. Concrete can hold water, but there is a chance it could crack so this vase has a glass inside that stays there even after unmolding. The glass holds the water, making the vessel safe to use for cut flowers.

YOU WILL NEED

...

large juice carton—mine held 3 pints (1.75 litres)

drinking glass, 5½ in (14cm) tall and 2¾ in (7cm) wide

ruler

pen

scissors

craft knife

strong tape

concrete mix—I used approximately 6½ lb (3kg)

safety goggles, gloves, and dust mask

paint—I used Annie Sloan Chalk Paint in Henrietta, mixed with a touch of white

paintbrush

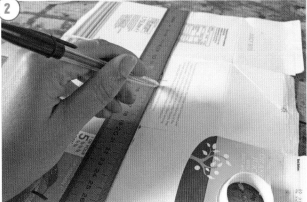

1 Open the juice carton into a flat piece by opening out the joins at the top and down the side. Cut out the base and set aside. I was then left with a flat piece of card measuring 11 x 10¼ in (28 x 26cm).

2 Using the ruler and pen, mark the middle of the carton by drawing a horizontal line from one upright side across to the other.

3 Measure along the top and bottom edges of the carton and make a mark at the top and bottom of your carton every 3½ in (9cm).

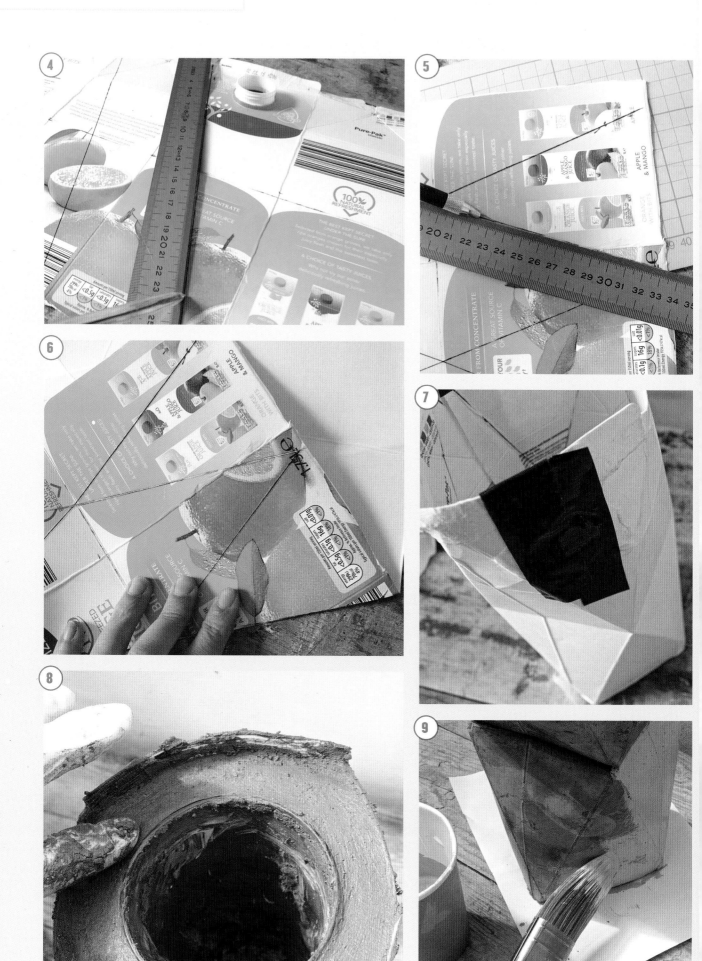

4 Connect the top corner with the first mark at the bottom of your carton by drawing a diagonal line. Working your way across the carton in one direction, draw another set of diagonal lines in the other direction.

5 Score over the diagonal lines and the horizontal line with the craft knife, but don't cut too deep—you just want to make it easier to fold the carton, not cut it in two.

6 Fold all the scored lines, pressing them down well with your fingers to create creases in the carton.

7 When all the lines are folded, reassemble the carton back but this time it should be inside out so the folded shapes show nicely. Use strong tape to keep the seam together. If your carton had a plastic spout, cut this out and cover the hole with tape. Tape the base in place as well. Check the seams are strong enough by pouring water in the vase—if it leaks, add more tape.

8 Mix the concrete according to the packet instructions (also see page 9) and fill the mold two-thirds full. Push the drinking glass into the middle of the concrete, then add a bit more concrete to the mold if necessary to ensure the concrete is level with the top of the glass. Smooth the top with your fingers and tap the sides to release any air bubbles. If the glass rises up, weigh it down with nails or coins.

9 When the concrete is completely hard (this will take a day or so), peel away the tape and carefully remove the carton. Paint the vase any color you like—I mixed Annie Sloan Chalk Paint in Henrietta with a bit of white paint.

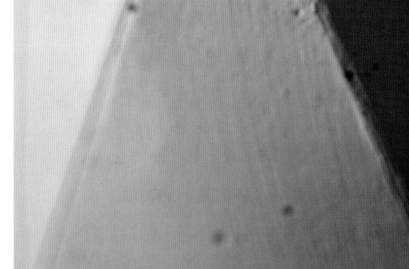

DISPLAY TRIANGLE

• • •

This triangle is a great decorative storage piece. Make a couple and hang them on the wall to store treasured souvenirs, or have one resting on your mantelpiece to display some of your favorite books and ornaments. You might even get creative and make a circle or square as well—a selection of shapes would look great hung on the wall in a hallway.

YOU WILL NEED

• • •

three pieces of wood, 2 in (5cm) wide and 24 in (60cm) long

measuring rule

saw

screws and screwdriver

piece of styrofoam/polystyrene, 15 x 15 in (38 x 38cm) and 2 in (5cm) thick

glue

flat surface, such as a piece of plywood, larger than the wooden frame

silicon sealant

concrete mix—I used approximately 10 lb (4.5kg) of a coarse type

safety goggles, gloves, and dust mask

putty knife

craft knife

sandpaper

1 Cut the wood to size and place the three pieces in a triangular shape. Three of the ends will need to be cut at an angle of 45° (see the photo below), so measure and mark the ends where you need to cut. Saw at an angle as marked.

2 Screw the three sides of the triangle together.

3 Cut the styrofoam into a triangle that is smaller than the internal dimensions of the wooden triangle. I left a gap of 2 in (5cm) between the wood and styrofoam (the thicker the sides, the stronger your triangle will be). Apply some glue to one side of the styrofoam and stick it centrally to the flat surface. Place the wooden triangle on the board, ensuring it is placed equidistantly and glue in place with sealant. Let the sealant harden for an hour.

4 Mix the concrete according to the packet instructions (also see page 9) and press it firmly into the gap. Fill the mold completely, making the top as smooth as possible. Don't worry that some concrete will spread over the styrofoam.

5 Let the concrete harden for a few days—this is a fragile build so be sure to give it enough time. When dry, cut the sealant away with a craft knife, then unscrew the mold. Carefully prise the wood away from the concrete. Using a putty knife, slowly prise the concrete away from the flat surface—be very careful as it is fragile.

6 Using a craft knife, cut the styrofoam into smaller pieces and press them out of the concrete triangle. Clean all the bits of styrofoam away and sand away any rough edges.

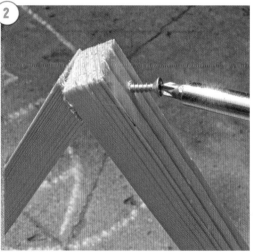

BOOKEND

• • •

The weight of concrete makes it a perfect medium for bookends. Cast them in any letter you wish—spell out a word, your initials, or, as here, the letter "B" for book. Plain-colored letters would be fun, but I made mine a little more interesting by marbling the concrete mix. Adding a little splash of food coloring means you can introduce a pop of color to your bookshelves. You won't know how the color has taken until after you release the mold, making the unmolding process very exciting! It is important to make the cardboard mold in reverse, as the flat underside will form the front of the letter.

YOU WILL NEED

• • •

strips of cardboard 3½ in (9cm) wide—for the letter B I used four strips 7 in (18cm), 8¾ in (22cm), 10 in (25cm), and 20 in (50cm) long

measuring tape

scissors

stapler

parcel tape

a flat surface, such as a piece of wood or board

glue gun

concrete mix—I used approximately 2¾ lb (1.2kg)

safety goggles, gloves, and dust mask

food coloring

old spoon

sandpaper

protective cork pads

1 Fold the two shorter pieces of cardboard into oval shapes and staple together. These will form the holes or spacers in the upper and lower sections of the letter B.

2 Wrap the two remaining lengths of cardboard and the two spacers in parcel tape, making the cardboard water resistant.

3 Tape the two long lengths of cardboard together at both ends, making one circular piece, and bend it into a B. The shorter of these two pieces will become the straight upright and the longer piece will form the curve that makes the B shape.

4 Glue the spacers to the flat board using the hot glue gun (the larger spacer appears at the bottom of the letter B). Glue the longer piece to the board in a B shape. Make sure that the cardboard edge which will form the base of the bookend is as straight as possible to prevent the finished bookend wobbling, and remember to make the letter in reverse.

5 Add some drops of food coloring to the base of the mold.

6 Mix the concrete according to the packet instructions (also see page 9) and swirl in some more food coloring. Don't over-mix as you want the color to produce a marbled effect. Spoon the mix into the mold—using a spoon gives you more control over where the color appears. Smooth the concrete with your fingers or spoon and tap the sides of the mold to release any air bubbles. Let dry.

7 When the concrete is completely hard (this may take a day or so), carefully peel the cardboard away from the letter. Prise the letter away from the board and smooth away any rough edges with sandpaper.

8 Glue protective cork pads to the bottom of the bookend so that it doesn't scratch your bookshelves.

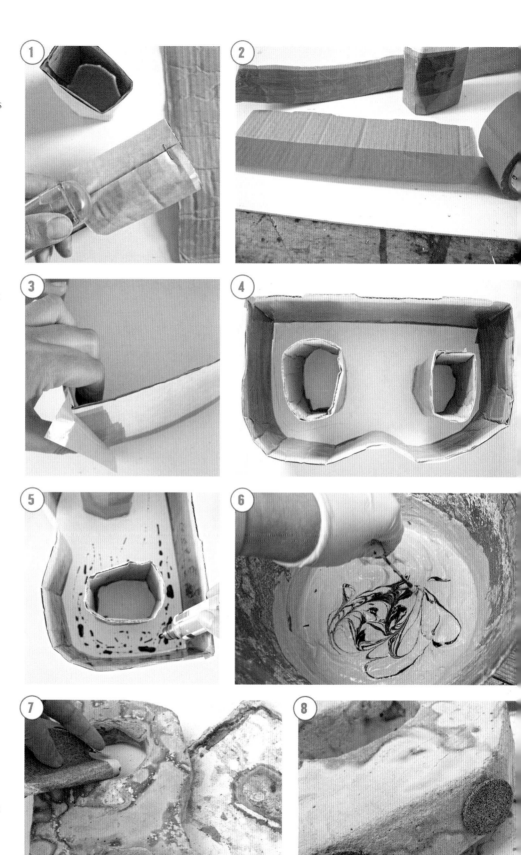

PATTERNED VASE

• • •

Would you believe me when I say that this vase is super simple to make, despite all the intricate details? The lovely pattern is created by an embossed silicon sheet placed inside the mold. These silicon fondant mats are used for creating delicate patterns on wedding cakes, but they are great for concrete too! You can buy large sheets online or have a look in your local kitchen shop (just make sure the flexible sheet is larger or the same size as the vase you want to make). The glass inside the vase makes it safe to use for stem flowers, but you can use it as a planter for something like a cactus or succulent, which requires little watering so there is no need for a drainage hole.

YOU WILL NEED
...

wooden planks—see step 1 for sizes

measuring rule

saw

drill plus wood bit

screws and screwdriver

silicon sealant

silicon fondant mat—I used a sheet measuring 12 x 16 in (30 x 40cm)

scissors

concrete mix—I used approximately 3¼ lb (1.5kg)

safety goggles, gloves, and dust mask

beige pigment for concrete—I used 3½ oz (100g) of York buff from Cemcraft

glass jar or drinking glass that fits easily in the mold

nails or coins, to use as a weight

craft knife

putty knife

sandpaper

1 Cut the wood for the mold to size. You need two side pieces 4 x 8 in (10 x 20cm), another two side pieces 4 in (10cm) x [8 in (20cm) + twice the thickness of wood], and one base piece 4 x 4 in (10 x 10cm).

2 Construct the mold. Drill and screw the two shorter side pieces to opposite sides of the base, then attach the two longer side pieces. Seal all the side and base joints with silicon sealant.

3 Place the silicon mat inside the mold and cut away any extra silicon—you want the mat to sit inside the mold as flat as possible.

4 Mix the concrete powder with the pigment, then add water according to the packet instructions (also see page 9). Pour the concrete into the mold until it is two-thirds full. Tap the sides of the mold to release any air bubbles.

5 Push the glass jar into the middle of the mold, so the top of the jar is level with the concrete. Weigh the jar down with nails to prevent it floating up. Let the concrete set—this will take a day or so.

6 When the concrete has set, unscrew the mold and cut the silicon sealant away. Remove the wood from around the concrete. Peel the silicon mat away from the vase, revealing the delicate pattern.

7 Using a putty knife, prise the vase away from its wooden base. Sand away any rough edges.

PHONE CHARGING STATION

• • •

Never know where your phone is? Join the club! I always seemed to misplace mine, but with this stylish charging station that is a thing of the past. As soon as I walk through the door, I place my phone in the charging slot and put my keys in the space next to them. The extra slot is also great for coins. If you prefer the charging station to be next to your bed, keep your jewelry in the second slot or maybe a set of headphones. I suggest buying a spare plastic-coated charging cable for this build—something bright like this blue one looks great against the gray of the concrete.

YOU WILL NEED
...

empty 35 fl oz (1 litre) juice carton

ruler

pen

craft knife

scissors

duct tape or similarly strong tape

phone charging cable

electrical tape

concrete mix—I used approximately
2 lb (900g)

safety goggles, gloves, and dust mask

offcuts of wood or something flat, such
as a book

nails or coins, to use as a weight

sandpaper

1 Place the juice carton on its side and draw a line 2⅜ in (6cm) from one long side. Cut around the line on all four sides of the carton to create the base mold.

2 The leftover piece of carton will be used to create an inner mold. Open out this piece of the carton and lay it flat (this flattened piece of carton needs to be at least 6¾ x 4¾ in/17x12cm). Place your phone upright in the middle of the flattened carton and draw around it.

3 Using a craft knife, score a rectangle ¼ in (5mm) outside the rectangle drawn around the phone.

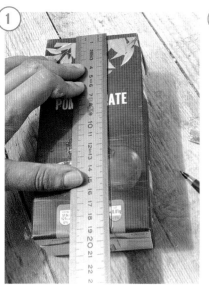

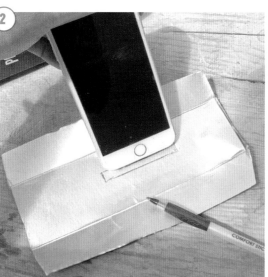

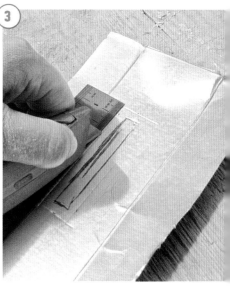

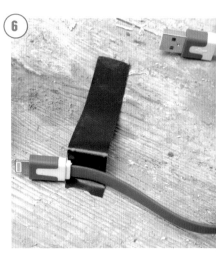

4 Using scissors, make diagonal cuts from the four corners of the carton to the corners of scored rectangle.

5 Fold the carton into a little box, using duct tape to secure the sides in place.

6 Wrap electrical tape around the piece of the charging cable that will sit in the concrete—this will be roughly the first 2 in (5cm) from the plug.

7 Make a second smaller inner mold following steps 2–5, using leftover pieces of juice carton or use another one. The second mold needs to be roughly 2⅜ x 1½ in (6 x 4cm) and 1¼ in (3cm) high.

8 Cut a slit in one long side of the first inner mold and push the charging cable through, so that only the plug

(rather than any cable) comes out on the inside. Put duct tape around the plug to close the slit, as you don't want concrete to seep through.

9 On the large outer mold mark where the lead will come out of the mold and make a slit. Push the lead through and close the slit on the outside with duct tape so no concrete can leak out.

10 Mix your concrete according to the packet instructions (also see page 9). Stand the outer mold upright with the charging cable and inner mold in place. Fill the space around two-thirds full.

11 To keep the sides straight and prevent them bowing out, place the two pieces of wood around the mold and keep them in place with tape. If you don't have any wooden offcuts, use books or serving trays.

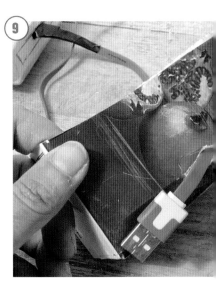

12 Push the charger mold down into the concrete. If necessary, put some masking tape around the plug to protect it from any concrete spilling into the mold. Also push the second smaller inner mold in place. Keep both from floating up by weighing them down with nails or coins.

13 When the concrete has set (this will take a day or so), open the carton on all sides. Remove the tape and carefully cut the mold away from the charging cable.

14 Pull out the small inner mold— it should release easily when you squeeze the sides together. Carefully cut the mold open around the plug and remove. Sand away any rough edges.

CONCRETE PHOTO ART

• • •

How great do these photos printed on concrete look? They give an industrial edge to your favorite family snaps, make your childhood memories look even cooler, and make great gifts. My concrete photos are postcard sized but you can make your artworks bigger or smaller. As long as you can print it, you can concrete photo art it! Photos with bright colors on a dark background will show up best on the concrete, but I also really like the faded look a black-and-white print gives. Have a play around to find which look you like best, but you might want to boost the color, saturation, and contrast of your image for a better print. With the black-and-white image, I increased the contrast for a better print.

TIP

• • •

You might want to make a couple of concrete slabs as if something goes wrong with the printing part (you have to place the photo on the concrete in one smooth move, no adjusting possible), you have to wait a day until you have new slabs ready for printing.

YOU WILL NEED

...

wooden baton, 27 in (68cm) long
—mine is ¾ x 1⅛ in (18 x 28mm),
but you can use any offcuts you
may have

measuring rule

saw

4 screws

screwdriver

flat surface, such as a floorboard,
piece of laminate, or a plastic lid

silicone sealant

concrete mix—I used
approximately 1 lb 2 oz (500g)

safety goggles, gloves, and
dust mask

plastic spatula

craft knife

sandpaper

sheet of self-adhesive labels

printer

clear varnish

paintbrush

1 Start by building a frame. Cut your baton into four pieces 6¾ in (17cm) long and screw together to build your frame. Place the frame on a flat surface (I used an old laminate board) and use silicon sealant to stick in place.

2 Mix your concrete according to the packet instructions (also see page 9) and pour it into the frame. Smooth the concrete as much as you can with a plastic spatula. Lift the board up slightly and let it fall gently back onto the table— this will release any air bubbles and level the concrete. Let the concrete set until fully hardened (this will take at least half a day).

3 Carefully cut the sealant away with a craft knife. Unscrew the frame and pull the batons away from the concrete. Sand away any rough edges.

4 Using a photo-editing program on your computer, flip your chosen image horizontally and size your picture: for a full photo on this size of frame you'll need 5⅛ x 6¾ in (13 x 17cm) or for a square Polaroid look 4 x 4 in (10 x 10cm).

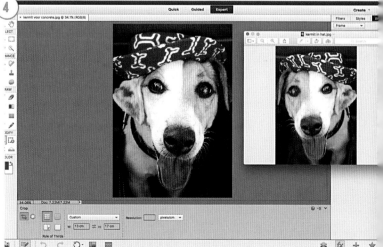

5 Remove all the labels from a printable sticky label sheet, then put the empty sheet in your printer so it prints on the shiny side of the paper. Print your image and be very careful handling the photo as the ink will not set on the paper—don't touch it and don't drop it or the floor will have a photo printed on it!

6 Place the print ink side down on the concrete slab. This has to be placed in one smooth move. You can't rearrange the print due to the wet ink— once it's down, it's down. Fear not as a wonky print can look very nice as well!

7 Rub over the image, making sure you don't move the paper, to transfer the image from the paper to the concrete.

8 Peel off the paper to reveal your newly printed concrete slab. Let the ink dry for a few minutes.

9 To protect the ink from fading, apply a coat of clear varnish, preferably a matt one.

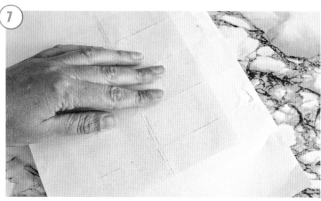

STORAGE JAR

• • •

This jar is great to hold your treats, whether they are chocolates, cookies, or cat biscuits! Made from a supermarket dessert container, I love the swirls the packaging gave the sides. The jar has a lid made from a wooden circle that slots into the neck of the jar. A lick of yellow paint finishes the storage jar off—a pop of color for when your treats are finished. My jar is of a medium size, but you can make yours a lot smaller or bigger if you wish—just use a different size of container as a mold.

YOU WILL NEED

• • •

plastic pudding bowl, 6 in (15cm) wide and 3¼ in (8cm) high

plastic bowl, 4¾ in (12cm) wide and 3¼ in (8cm) high

paper

pen

cooking spray

concrete mix—I used approximately 1 lb 2 oz (500g)

safety goggles, gloves, and dust mask

nails or coins, to use as a weight

sandpaper

yellow paint—I used Annie Sloan Chalk Paint in English Mustard

paintbrush

scissors

wood—I used scrap pieces of ¼ in (7mm) ply and ⅝ in (16mm) pine board

saw or jigsaw

piece of dowel, ⅝ in (15mm) wide and 1 in (2.5cm) long

drill with wood drill bit

screw

clear varnish

1 Place the pudding bowl (which forms the outer mold) and smaller bowl (the inner mold) upside down on a piece of paper and trace around the rims. Keep to one side as you will use these templates to make the lid later.

2 As my mold has a lot of swirls on the sides, I used cooking spray to make it easier to release the concrete. Spray a little on the inside walls of the outer mold and a little on the outer walls of the inner mold.

3 Mix your concrete according to the packet instructions (also see page 9) and fill the mold half full. Push the inner mold into the concrete, leaving it about ½ in (1cm) higher than than the outer mold. Tap the sides of the mold to release any air bubbles.

4 To stop the inner mold rising up, weigh it down with nails or coins. Let the concrete set for a day or so.

5 When the concrete has hardened, pull out the inner mold. It should come loose with just a wiggle; if not, cut the inner mold open. Place the outer mold upside down and the concrete pot should just slide out; if not, cut it open.

6 Sand away any rough edges. Paint the inside of the jar a bright color and let dry. Apply a second coat if necessary.

7 To make the lid, cut out the circles drawn on the paper and make sure they are still the same size as your bowl. The bigger circle should be the same size as the rim of the jar and the small circle should just fall inside the jar. Adjust your paper templates if necessary.

8 Place the circles on the pieces of wood and draw around them. I used a thicker wood for the larger circle and a thinner piece for the smaller circle. Cut out the circles and sand away any rough edges.

9 Mark the middle on both wooden circles. The easiest way to do this is to fold the paper templates into quarters, cut off the tip and line that up on the wooden circles. Drill through the circles on the marks you have made.

10 Also predrill a hole in the middle of the piece of dowel, making sure you don't drill deeper than ⅓ in (8mm). Join the three pieces together by screwing through the small circle, then through the large circle and into the dowel.

11 Paint the wooden lid yellow. I thinned the paint with a spoonful of water as I like to see the grain of the wood on the lid. Allow to dry thoroughly. Also give the bowl a coat of clear varnish to ensure that no concrete dust will get on your food.

RESOURCES

• • •

www.hestershandmadehome.com
www.youtube.com/handmadehome
Instagram: byhestergrams
Twitter: hestershandmade
Facebook: hestershandmadehome

CONCRETE AND CEMENT

For this book I've used:
• Everbuilt Jetcem, rapid set concrete, www.everbuild. com/jetcem
• Hanson Castle white cement, www.hanson.co.uk
• Hanson Instant concrete and Multi purpose concrete, www.hanson.co.uk
• Polycell quick set cement, www.polycell.co.uk
• Carlton FP-ECOFIX rapid set fence post concrete, www.carltonmanufacturing.co.uk
• Blue Circle postcrete, www.wickes.com
• These are for sale instore or online, such as www.diy. com and www.wickes.com

In the USA try:
Quikrete, www.quikrete.com
Sakrete, www.sakrete.com
Cheng-pro formula mix, www.concreteexchange.com

PIGMENTS AND PAINT

Colored pigments by Cemcraft, www.cemcraft.com
Chalk paint by Annie Sloan, www.anniesloan.com
Tile paint by Wilko, www.wilko.com

ITEMS USED IN VARIOUS PROJECTS

• All yarn used is Zpagetti yarn by Hoooked, www.hoooked.co.uk
• Doilies can be bought in charity/thrift shops and oohmycraft Ebay shop
• Ceramic gas fire pebbles are from www.coals4u.com
• Candle inserts by The Norfolk Candle Company, www.norfolkcandleco.co.uk
• LED festoon outdoor party lights by Lights4fun, www.lights4fun.co.uk
• Mosaic tiles in craft shops like www.hobbycraft. co.uk or www.mosaicsupplies.co.uk
• Copper pipes and connector pieces at Wickes, www. wickes.co.uk
• Door handles used as tray handles from Wickes, www.wickes.co.uk

• Flexible plastic tubs for mixing and pouring from DIY or garden centers, such as www.homebase.co.uk or www.homedepot.com
• Pump from Sunspray (SE 360 fountain), available in garden centers and online
• XL ice cube trays available online or in kitchen shops
• Turtle toy by Wilko, www.wilko.com
• Silicon sugar craft mats and silicon cake molds can be found in kitchen shops and craft stores, or at www.lakeland.co.uk
• Crockery used in shots is Falcon ware, www.falconenamelware.com
• All flowers and succulents by Etc. Margate, www.etcetera-online.co.uk

INSPIRATIONS

I'm a magazine junkie and some of my fave titles and blogs are:
• www.kinfolk.com: beautiful photography and inspiring interiors.
• www.thesimplethings.com: this magazine is all about taking time to live well and enjoy the small things in life.
• www.marthastewart.com: the queen bee of crafting, Martha Stewart Living magazine should be on every crafter's reading list.
• www.bhg.com: the amazing Do It Yourself magazine is part of the Better Homes and Garden group and is great for DIY tips and ideas.
• www.vtwonen.nl: Dutch interior and DIY magazine which features toned-down Dutch design.
• www.sweetpaulmag.com: I love this magazine and blog, always full of great ideas and tips.
• www.homeandgarden.nl: another great Dutch title full of inspiration for outdoor living.
• readcereal.com: stunning photography and travel inspiration.
• www.abeautifulmess.com: Elsie and Emma have such a fresh and unique approach to home decor and crafts.
• blog.westelm.com: the Front+Main blog from interior mastermind West Elm.
• www.instagram.com: you can glimpse inside the lives of crafter-makers all over the world.

LOCATIONS

The book was shot in Hester's house, Etc. in Margate, and 26 Harbour Street, Ramsgate.

INDEX

• • •

AUTHOR'S ACKNOWLEDGMENTS
....

Thanks to:
• Cindy and Penny for giving me another book.
• Sally, Anna, Gillian, and Kerry for editing and all other help, and Elizabeth for her great book design.

• A massive cheer for James Gardiner, who once again shot all the lovely project images.
• Ian for the countless trips to the DIY store to purchase even more concrete and his modeling skills.
• Shelly, and her staff, for letting me use her beautiful shop Etc.
• Ben and Tracey for letting me shoot in

their bar before it even opened and for being my background models.
• Annie Sloan and her team for their paint selection.
• Andrew and Molly for coming over to model after a long day's work.
• And my sister for FaceTime calls whenever concrete and I didn't get on ;)